Yes

Courtney Koctar

TO JT, WYATT, ANITA & KAKURU

There would be no story without the four of you.

CONTENTS

ACKNOWLEDGMENTS

I want to thank Netflix for occupying my children while I wrote this book. It would not have been possible without you. Yes, we are still watching.

1

IT'S TIME

We always knew we would adopt children. Well, I did. When I was little, and I envisioned my family someday the only thing I knew was that my kids were not going to look like me. I used to tell my parents, "I'm going to marry someone from Texas, and I'm going to have black kids one day." I can't explain it. I just knew. Then I married Dustin, who is a white male when we were both twenty-two years old. He is from Texas, so one out of two ain't bad, right? We decided we would adopt one day, one day being the keywords in that sentence. Like, when we were thirty or something and definitely after we had traveled to Italy.

We spent those early years living life as a broke, young married couple. We worked jobs and did grad school. We made new friends in the city I was raised in. We barely paid our bills. We ate so much pasta because a box only cost ninety-nine cents and could feed us for days. We even bought pasta in different shapes to make us feel like we were eating something different because we were so broke and fancy like that. We quit jobs and got new ones. We moved in with my parents for a season. We moved out. We took so many road trips. We fought and argued and slammed doors. We ran half marathons together. We Googled divorce once because marriage can be really stupid. We laughed and cried and dreamed together. We were so young; two kids who were coming together to figure out this dance called forever.

One night we sat outside on the balcony of our apartment complex dreaming about what we wanted the year 2012 to look like. We both wanted to run another half marathon together. He wanted to take guitar lessons, and I wanted to take cooking classes. We wanted to serve somewhere together, and we wanted to leave the country for a minute. We wanted adventure. We didn't know then what any of this would look like or how it would all play out, but we made our list and set out to make it happen.

He did take guitar lessons, and I can tell you cooking classes are wildly fun. I can't remember where we ran a race that year, but I know we ran it. Then we found ourselves packing up our bags and heading to Uganda, a place I could not have pointed to on a map before that trip, and it changed our lives. If that sounds dramatic, it's because it is. We wanted adventure, and an adventure is what we got. Be careful what you wish for.

We spent a month living in a village with some of the most

precious people on this planet Earth. We ate what they ate and lived as they lived. It was the first time I had left the country and not stayed in a Marriot hotel. We climbed in bed every night through the opening in our mosquito net and fell asleep to the sounds of Uganda. We found a lizard in our bed once. We woke up every morning to the sound of the rooster crowing and Mary asking us, "How were your dreams" in a slightly creepy voice with her big eyes staring deep into your soul. The only kind of cabbage I now like is the kind we had at Faith's house that summer. We learned how to make the perfect cup of black tea. Dustin killed a chicken with a dull knife one day and then we ate it for dinner that night. We stayed up late playing cards by flashlight because the electricity never worked when you needed it to.

We lived for a month with no running water. When it was time to take a shower we were handed one bucket of cold water; the women would laugh when we requested the water to be heated up over the fire. I now know what a "squatty potty" is; it is a hole in the ground, and it is your bathroom. Do not fall in. I can tell you that the only times you want to use the bathroom are early mornings or in the middle of the night. Because when your bathroom is a hole of crap that sits on the equator it all becomes somewhat offensive to your senses, say around noon.

We didn't do anything for anyone on that trip. We merely lived life alongside people who were living an extremely different life than we were back home. It was a sweet month. We fell in love with Uganda. The people are beautiful- kind and generous. The country is stunning- the rolling, green hills and the red dirt that stays on you forever. I sobbed when we left.

A year after that trip, we were sitting on our front porch drinking coffee. For a while, I had been feeling this weird nudge. I had heard this little whisper in my ear. I felt this pull on my heart... It's time. We were twenty- five. We weren't ready. I was adamant about not discussing children before we were thirty. We were so young. We had so many things we still needed to do. We still needed to travel to Italy for crying out loud. I pushed that nudge down and told it not yet. I waved that whisper away in the name of I'm not thirty yet. I told the pull on my heart we'd do it one day. What I know now is that was the Holy Spirit... that nudge, the whisper, the pull. I've learned the Holy Spirit is like a fly that won't leave you the heck alone. You know the kind. You can wave your hand around like a complete lunatic, but that thing keeps coming back buzzing around your face. That's the Holy Spirit to me, and it wouldn't leave me alone. I had waved it away for a long time in secret, and I couldn't wave it away anymore. It was time. That day on our porch I took a deep breath, refused to make eye contact with my husband and blurted out, "I think we're supposed to adopt from Uganda, and I think we're supposed to do it now." His exact response, "I think we are too."

We didn't tell anyone. We asked a few friends to simply pray for us as we navigated the idea and did research and had conversations, but we weren't officially adopting, not yet. It was all extremely overwhelming and wildly terrifying. I will never forget the night two friends randomly showed up on our front porch. They handed over an envelope and said, "This is leftover money we had

4

budgeted for our trip to Italy. We want you guys to have it as you start the adoption process." I walked back into our house that night completely stunned. We weren't even legitimately doing anything right then. I was still all kinds of petrified of the whole thing. We hadn't asked for any money because we weren't adopting but yet we had been handed an envelope and told to do it. I learned that evening God could prompt you to do something that feels intimidating. He can tell you do something and give you no clear game plan. He can ask you to do something that honestly makes no logical sense and leaves you with one million unanswered questions. And while you stand in the middle of the whole ordeal wavering, he can meet you right on your front porch, hand you an envelope when you never asked him for an envelope and invite you to trust him. I got yes tattooed on my right wrist not long after this. I remember the night I got it. It felt holy, getting this declaration on my skin that was beating in my heart. We were stepping out in faith. We were taking a risk. We were doing something scary. We were trying to be obedient in the midst of the unknown. We were doing something big. We were saying yes.

But here's the thing about saying yes, you say it, and then you have to move. I didn't know this at the time. Saying yes doesn't do one thing for you. Saying yes is not some magic word that makes everything make sense or fall into place. It's not a snap of a finger and poof there you have it. Saying yes is just that, saying a word, but doing yes is something entirely different. We like to talk about saying yes with our lives in the same way we like to talk about eating healthy. It sounds nice until you're craving copious amounts of bread and cheese and ice cream. But eating healthy requires you to shop differently at the grocery store and stop driving through Sonic for corn dogs. It demands action. It requires you to move with your feet. So does saying yes.

Adoption is tricky. I want to say this. It is complicated and nuanced and complex. Kids' best interests are not always a priority. Adoptive parents do not always care about ethics. They do not always do their due diligence. Adoption agencies don't either. Domestic or international, it doesn't matter. Then you try to navigate the international world of orphanages and, news flash, they don't always care about ethics either. Adoption is a business whether anyone wants to awkwardly acknowledge it or not, it very much is.

We were well aware a lot of children living in orphanages across the globe did have living parents who just could not afford to take care of them. We didn't want to parent those kids. We felt so strongly that was not our job. We wanted to parent kids who had no other option, no other chance at a family. We searched and searched for an adoption agency that first and foremost believed in ethics and second of all believed in finding families for kids not finding kids for families because there is a very distinct difference. We never set out to be white saviors. We were not adopting to rescue or save a child because there was nothing to rescue or save them from. It grieved us deeply to think this child would be losing their native language and home country and everything they ever knew. We reasoned that if and only if there was a need, then we were available. We never wanted to parent someone else's child just because we had the money to feed them. We believe that kids belong in their biological families first. We said from the beginning; we only wanted to adopt a child who had no other options because no child belongs in an institution forever.

And then one day we found ourselves formally adopting from Uganda. All the paperwork was filled out, the classes had been taken, the books were being read, and we just waited. I remember the day I sat at work and got the email with his picture attached to it. His story was hard to read, it was sad, but his eyes looked happy, they sparkled. I've learned since then that not all living kid's eyes look happy; not all children's eyes look alive. We were asked to talk and pray about being his family, but I knew immediately. I felt it in my soul. It felt daunting and thrilling; I knew in my gut it was right to say yes to him and we did. We were going to have a son.

I've learned that saying yes is risky. It's scary. Saying yes is hard. It's also super brave. Saying yes means showing up. Saying yes is doing the hard thing not sure if it will work out. Saying yes means telling the truth- the ugly, messy, beautiful truth. Saying yes is inviting pain and sorrow and brokenness into your story. Saying yes is courageous. Saying yes means doing the scary thing afraid. Saying yes means going terrified.

I look back at that twenty-five-year-old woman, and I want to hug her. I want to sit her down, pour her a cup of coffee and tell her: *You have no idea what is coming, sister. You are about to live some life and experience some pain. You are going to do impossibly hard things in the years to come. You are going to have to be brave. You are going to want to say no. Some days you may regret your yes, but you are going to say yes a lot of times and every time will be right, ugly, messy, hard, and beautiful. You've got grit, girl. You do. I've seen it. Keep saying yes. Your life is going to be everything and nothing like what you had imagined it would be.*

2

JT

Dustin and I spent months staring at his pictures. We knew his smile like we knew the back of our hands. He looked like a total mess. He looked spunky. He looked hilarious. He looked happy. We wondered what his voice sounded like, what his laugh was like. We spent months praying for him by name, JT. We prayed he was healthy, loved, and cared for. We prayed for this upcoming transition. We prayed for grace and understanding; we prayed for protection over his little heart.

We spent months preparing for him. We painted his bedroom blue. I stood in Walmart for an embarrassing amount of time trying to decide on that perfect color. We put little boy sheets on his bed, and I dreamed about kissing him goodnight and watching him sleep. Friends threw us baby showers. We washed and hung up his clothes. I could imagine all the dirt and stains and bloody knees we would have one day. We bought toys and hoped he liked cars and balls. Dustin went to the bookstore one afternoon and came home with bags of books he had picked out just for him. We talked about him daily. We wondered what it was all going to be like. We started to let ourselves dream of him being in our home; playing baseball, riding bikes, going swimming, reading bedtime stories. We began to dream of being a family.

The only thing left to do was go. I remember the night we sat on our ugly, plaid sofa and booked our plane tickets. My heart was beating out of my chest, and we both buzzed with child-like energy. This was it; this was the long awaited for final step. I would head over by myself and Dustin would follow a few weeks later. It was a fool-proof plan. We let out the breath we had been holding for months and gasped for air as if we had been underwater for too long. We finally felt safe, like nothing could happen at this point. Several weeks later, I found myself boarding an airplane in the direction of Uganda to go and be with that little boy who would become my son. I would do the things that needed to be done in Uganda, and then I would board a plane out of Uganda in a few months with that little boy beside me. It was how it all worked, and it felt exciting; like this crazy act of obedience was about to have a happy ending.

I remember driving down the red dirt road that led up to his orphanage. I was nervous and excited; I was about to become a mom. I got out of the van and was ushered back into an office where I waited with my social worker. It all felt so holy, this moment of honoring all this little boy had lost in his short life and holding space for gains. The next thing I knew, a little boy bounded into the room, and I heard, "JT! This is your new mom!" He jumped up in my lap, this bundle of three-year-old energy and started talking a mile a minute in a language I couldn't understand, and I thought, "This is going to be good."

It turns out he was indeed spunky, a total mess and hilarious. He did love balls. His laugh made me die a little. He had an infectious smile, that boy. His eyes were full of such joy. He loved to be tickled and chased and flipped upside down. He would climb trees and jump out of them. He loved to color. He was a good friend, and he was kind. He loved to hold my hand. He called me mommy. The way to his heart was chapati (think if Jesus made a tortilla) and jackfruit. He told me he loved me, and he most likely didn't, this boy who didn't know the first thing about me except that I was his new mom. I told him I loved him and I did, this little boy who I didn't know the first thing about except that he was going to be my son.

I will never forget standing in my house in Uganda and getting the phone call that shattered my heart into a million pieces. The unimaginable words being uttered on the other end of the phone saying to me, "I'm so sorry, Courtney. This has never happened before. We can't continue to pursue this adoption ethically." And just like that, it was over. The details will always remain private, but after all the investigations and work that had been done to prevent something like this, it happened. There was nothing we could do, ethics matter; we knew we had to walk away. I dialed Dustin's number as tears fell down my face and choked out what was happening thousands of miles across the globe. It was the most painful, matter of fact conversation of my entire life. I was on the next flight out of Uganda headed back home sans little boy. It was utterly devastating. It was right to walk away, and it was also devastating.

I flippantly opened my Bible that night looking for something, anything, to ease the pain I felt in my insides. I desperately wanted God to reveal himself to me in this moment of heartache. I wanted him to give me an answer, a revelation that would make all of this make sense. Instead, he gave me Isaiah 55. The words lay before me as another invitation to trust him, but this time the invitation came at an excruciating cost. The words were not a welcome balm to my aching soul; instead, they felt like daggers to my shocked, destroyed heart. I took in what the Lord had given me that night, "For my thoughts are not your thoughts, neither are your ways my ways," declares the Lord. "As the heavens are higher than the earth, so are my ways higher than your ways and my thoughts than your thoughts." I felt crushed. It turns out he wasn't going to give me an answer after all. There would be no sweet moment of understanding, just God and me. The thing that didn't make sense would continue to not make sense this side of heaven. The reality of that pricked a little. I closed my Bible that night in Uganda and wouldn't open it again for a very long time.

Before I left, I had to say goodbye. There were so many things I wanted to tell him, things I wanted to make sure he knew before I left, but we didn't speak the same language, and he was three. I've learned since then three-year-olds don't like to listen much. He had been told bits and pieces of what was happening, but he didn't understand. He wanted to keep the coloring book and crayons I brought for him; that was his only request, so I left them with him. I pulled him in for one last hug and whispered something into his ear I can't remember. Then I turned around and walked away for good. I later learned he told everyone once he finished coloring all of the pages in his coloring book his new mommy would come back to get him. I can't breathe when I think about the day he did finally finish coloring every last page in that book.

I went back to my house, packed our bags, gave all my neighbors hugs and drove silently to the airport. There was nothing to say. It didn't feel real. I could not begin to grasp what was happening. It all felt like a bizarre dream. I couldn't decide if I was angry or devastated or just plain sad. I felt like maybe I was all of those things and none of those things. I didn't know. But I boarded a plane out of Uganda that night not sure I would ever come back. I boarded that plane half believing I would go back for JT and half thinking I never wanted to step foot on this country's soil ever again.

I cried the whole way from Uganda to Brussels, and then I turned angry. My jaw clenched; my eyes could have killed you with one cold look. I grabbed my bags and pounded my way to security where an agent politely asked me to "Step aside" in a delightful accent. But grief is a funny thing, it cannot be contained, the only thing you can do with grief is live it. I snapped. I completely lost it. I locked eyes with him and yelled back, "I am so sorry sir, but I think you are the one who should step aside." Jesus be a fence.

I stormed to my terminal where I waited to board my next flight, and there was only one open seat available. I rolled my eyes and begrudgingly sat down beside a big, burly older gentleman who did not pick up my social cues because he started talking to me. He pulled out a picture of a woman and told me he had just buried his mother. She was in the middle of a pretty standard surgery when she died suddenly on the table. His eyes glistened as he shared stories of her with me. I choked out through sobs what I had just experienced not even forty-eight hours earlier. We laughed and cried as we waited to board the plane. As we gathered our stuff and walked towards the agent scanning the tickets, he looked me square in the eyes and said, "You are going to be okay. You aren't going to be okay right now or probably for a very long time but trust me, one day you will be okay." I felt numb.

I boarded my last plane home entirely in denial. None of this had happened. I wasn't even sure I had been to Africa. I was pretty sure Ashton Kutcher was going to pop out at any terminal I walked by and shout, "You've been punk'd!" And everything would suddenly make sense. But that didn't happen, and by the time I landed in Nashville, I thought I was actively dying. I rode down the escalator towards baggage claim limping and walked straight into a hug from my husband. He whispered, "I thought this would be different." *Yeah, me too.* This is what grief looks like with skin on.

We drove straight to my parent's lake house. I couldn't go

home yet. I could not walk into the house that had been prepared for a life it turns out we wouldn't have. Not yet. For days I sobbed and raged with fury, I was unstable. I looked at flights to return to Uganda and crawled under my covers unable to physically move. I thought I might do something destructive for fun in my spare time. I decided I was in the FBI and would fix this thing with my own brain since no one else seemed to be able to. I had boarded the roller coaster that is grief, and the thing about roller coasters is you can't just get off at any time. Roller coasters are made to be ridden until they arrive back at the platform. Such is grief.

Nobody knew I was home. I had left for Uganda weeks ago publicly but returned silently. I didn't know what to say. I didn't know how to tell people. I was embarrassed. I couldn't explain why I felt so sad. And so I hid in my house for weeks unable to leave for fear of seeing someone I knew. What would I even say should someone look at me quizzically and ask, "I thought you were supposed to be in Africa?" *I thought I was, too?* I could not form sentences around what had just happened. I couldn't form sentences not because I didn't have the words but because I didn't want it all to be real.

For weeks I couldn't shower or change my clothes or eat anything. I couldn't sleep. I felt unable to physically get up off my couch. Every time I walked past his room I wanted to vomit. Dustin had closed the door to his room before I came home and it remained that way for months. I would learn later the man who believed he was going to be a dad had walked into that blue room one night before I arrived back home, had sat in the rocking chair by his little boy's bed and silently wept over the boy who would never be his son. He walked out that night and shut the door. He would never go back into that room the way he left. For months I couldn't go in there. I couldn't face all of his stuff. What was I supposed to do with the life we had prepared for?

I refused to unpack my bags. For weeks I stepped over them every morning trying to get to the bathroom and every night trying to get back into bed. I just knew my phone was going to ring at any minute and someone was going to tell me to come back. I was going to hear the words: It was all an accident. There was a mistake. All of this was wrong. Come back! Come be with your son!

When that didn't happen, I died my hair a different color and refused to go to church. I uttered obscene sentences out of my mouth. I listened to Christmas music in March because it was the only thing that felt right and I ate peanut butter M&Ms for all of my meals unapologetically. I cussed freely and wailed when I wanted to. I was harsh and offended and pissed off. I hated everything and everyone. I decided we should take a trip to Cuba. I thought we needed to move houses. I was relentless. I painted the walls of my house and stripped and stained a coffee table. Then one day I sat on my couch and penned this email. I sobbed so violently it almost hurts to think about now. It was time to keep moving. I pressed send, took a shower, got dressed and went to eat lunch with my husband.

From: Courtney Koctar

To: Dustin Koctar, BCC: Everyone

Sent: Monday, March 31, 2014, 8:31 AM

Subject: Adoption Update

I have dreaded having to write this email. It's like the minute I press send, and everyone knows it makes all that has happened actually real; trying to put words to what happened feels seemingly impossible. We've gone back and forth as far as what we say and how much do we want people to know. There is a part of me that wants to tuck these weeks away in my heart and not let anyone near it, but we made this journey a public one, and so here we are.

Some things have happened that re-opened JT's case and makes it impossible for us to continue to pursue adopting him. This is something that could never have been foreseen and has left a lot of people stunned and speechless. It's no one's fault, and there is no one to blame. It just is. (I know this is so vague it's stupid, but I also know that is what we're sharing and that's all.)

To say we are completely heartbroken would be a gross understatement. It feels like I've been to battle and I've come back beaten and bruised. My heart feels like it has been ripped out and used as a trampoline. To love a child, you can do nothing for feels so utterly helpless. To love a child who will never be "yours" is gut-wrenching.

I wrote this the day I left Uganda. I share it because I feel like it somehow puts words to a situation that otherwise really doesn't have any.

JT,

I want you to know we are heartbroken, devastated. My heart is aching a deep ache I didn't know before now. I want you to know we are sad. We have cried more tears than I knew either one of us had in us.

I want you to know I am so angry. I'm angry at God because this makes no sense. I'm mad at your family. I'm mad you are being put through all kinds of things no three-year-old on this planet should have to experience. I'm mad because you were left once by someone you called mom and now it feels like I'm doing the same thing.

I want you to know I was so excited to get to take you to the airport to pick up Daddy. Like, I had it all pictured in my head, and it was the cutest. I want you to know the red bike at our house will always have your name written on it.

I want you to know you are important. You were created for a reason, and you can do and be anything you want. I want you to know there is a God and he loves you more than you could ever imagine. I pray you grow up to serve the same God we do. I pray you go where he leads you. You are going to do great things for the kingdom.

I want you to know you are special. You have a gentle spirit, and I loved watching you love on your friends. You love well, buddy. You are spunky, and I told Daddy often that we were in trouble with you. Don't you ever lose those qualities.

I want you to know you were worth it. I have no idea why we are now a part of each other's stories, but we are. I'm so glad. I wouldn't trade the heartache for not knowing you. I want you to know you were a leap of faith. You were a yes. I pray you say yes to the things Jesus puts on your heart.

I want you to know in our hearts you will always be our first child. You will forever be the first person to call us mommy and daddy, and you will forever and always have a piece of our hearts.

We aren't done adopting. We don't have to start over. We just go back to waiting for a new referral. Although right now I can't even think of another child and the thought of doing this all over again makes me want to run away. Will you pray for our hearts? And will you pray for my buddy, JT? That God will somehow redeem and restore every ounce of his story.

Thanks, friends.
xoxo, CK

3

THE GOSPEL OF ENTITLEMENT

When I pressed send on that email, I could no longer deny what had happened. It was real, it was the truth. I had to put one foot in front of the other and continue walking forward, trudging through the grief. A spark of rage had been lit, and I developed a violent anger I did not know existed within me. I felt like I was on fire. I was mad; cuss words flowed freely, and so did hot, angry tears. I said some hideous, horrible things out loud. My body was tense, my muscles never relaxed. My jaw remained clenched, and I would look down and find my fingernails digging into my palms. I started grinding my teeth in my sleep. I went on hard, fast runs where I made myself heave, and I got sunburned on purpose more than once simply because I wanted to feel something. I wanted to physically feel the way my heart felt; angry and hurt. I thundered through my days, it was unwise to cross me. I confronted people I would never have confronted before over stupid things. I got riled up and could not be brought back down to Earth. I honked my car horn and flipped people off while driving. I was irate.

Finding a voice for my anger was harder than I imagined it would be. I could not for the life of me say anything other than cuss words. I could not form coherent, adult sentences with real words; until one day I could, and I despised every last one of them.

I'm angry because this isn't fair. I'm angry because this doesn't make sense. I'm angry because this doesn't seem just. I'm angry because we didn't do anything wrong. I'm angry because this isn't what I signed up for. I'm angry because he should be my son. I'm angry because doors opened and God moved all for this? I'm angry because we obeyed and now we're hurt. I'm angry because I feel like we deserved a good ending to our yes to Jesus.

What I found underneath all that anger was the real and disgusting stuff of my heart. As I acknowledged out loud what I felt on the inside of my being God invited me to tango with him; as if he knew the only way forward for me would be forged through a wrestling match with The Almighty. We suited up and went after it.

I screamed and cussed at him, I ugly snot cried at him. I was so mad. It all felt so mean. I didn't understand why he would so clearly tell us to do something, make a way and then blow it all up in our faces. I felt hurt. I felt like we had been tricked. I told him I didn't know if I wanted to believe in a God who did stuff like this and I meant every word. I begged him to change the story, I knew he could do it with a snap of his finger and it felt so cruel when he chose not to. I desperately wanted to trust him, but I felt like I couldn't.

I discovered that I had never really believed in the true gospel of Jesus Christ that reeks of obedience and suffering, but rather this weird gospel of entitlement. This made up gospel that said, I stepped out in faith. I said yes. I obeyed. It was scary and hard to do that. Therefore I deserve a happy ending. I'm entitled for it all to work out. I have a right to it.

I cracked open my Bible for the first time since that night in Uganda months ago and was reminded of the truth. I poured over the stories where God had required obedience from people, and it hadn't made any sense. I devoured these stories as if I had never read them before. Really I hadn't, not in this way, not through the lens of obedience at all cost.

Shadrach, Meshach, and Abednego- The king tells these men to bow down and worship an image he has built, or they will be thrown into a furnace. They refuse because they fear the Lord more than they fear a fire. They know they will die and they disobey the law of the land anyways. The Lord required these three men to stand in a fiery furnace for him as an act of obedience, and they do. They are bound and thrown into the furnace where they should have gone immediately up in flames, but the Lord rescues them. He saves their lives that day, but the truth is that he didn't have to do that. He could have required them to die in the furnace that day as an act of obedience to him, and that would have been the end of their story, and it also would have been enough.

Abraham- The Lord commands him to sacrifice his son, and

Abraham does it. The same son He had given Sarah after years of infertility. Abraham walks Isaac, his beloved, long awaited for child, to the altar. He ties him up, lays him on top of the wood and picks up the knife to kill his boy. You cannot tell me this made complete sense to Abraham. Can you imagine having to go back home and tell Sarah what you had done? What a painful act of obedience. But obedience requires sacrifice and sometimes that looks like death. The angel of the Lord calls out and tells him to stop, but he didn't have to. The Lord could have required Abraham to go through with the task of slaying his son on an altar for him.

Mary- The Lord put a baby inside of her virgin body and required her to trust him. What a weird thing. She will raise the son of God and then watch him be crucified. Sometimes I forget Jesus Christ, the savior of the world, had an earthly mother who changed his diapers and wiped his snotty nose and kissed his boo-boos and woke up with him in the middle of the night when he couldn't sleep. She potty trained him and made him lunches and got him every last snack. She watched that boy of hers grow up right in front of her very eyes. Mary did the ordinary work of motherhood and then let her son die on mission.

Jonah- The Lord tells Jonah to go to Nineveh, but Jonah doesn't want to go to Nineveh. He doesn't like those people and doesn't think they deserve the Good News. So he chooses disobedience and boards a boat to the opposite of Nineveh but God has him thrown overboard as the result of a storm, and a fish swallows him whole. The fish spits Jonah out, and the Lord tells him to go to Nineveh and this time Jonah does.

On and on I trekked my way through, and I found the Bible to be full of stories that in some ways mirrored my own and it caused me to pause. The scriptures are bursting of people who obeyed God when it made no sense to do so. The scriptures are packed with stories where obedience resulted in severe, scary, hurtful stuff. There was story after story of people who counted the cost of obedience and obeyed anyhow. There was story after story of people who didn't want to obey but did it nonetheless. There was story after story of people who questioned what in the heck God was up to and why he would choose someone like themselves and yet God required obedience from them in spite of it all.

I loved it because these people didn't always understand or necessarily get it. They didn't always want to do what was being asked of them, and they most certainly did not always enjoy it. Look at the story of Job for crying out loud. Even Jesus Christ asked God if there was any other way to do this thing. The disciples, Jesus' closest friends, were not always on board with what Jesus was asking them to do. But one thing was for sure; the Bible was full of people who believed in God and followed Christ no matter what, no matter the outcome. Some of them did wildly crazy things, Moses and Joshua and Rahab and Esther. Not one story was precisely the same, but the common thread became each one stepped into their calling to be obedient in the moment they were handed no matter their circumstances. Each one committed to obedience not knowing what the end of their story would be. I was reminded there is nothing about the gospel of Jesus Christ that is safe. The scriptures sing of obedience, risk, betrayal, pain, and suffering. These are at the core of the gospel. Jesus himself experienced each of these during his last days.

I don't know why I spent time on another continent with a little boy I thought would one day be my son. Were those days purposed? Was anything happening behind the scenes during that time? Was there spiritual warfare or a fight going on up in heaven over a little boy in Uganda? Or was it still and quiet? Were we hurt on purpose? Were we hurt as a punishment? Where was God in all of this? I don't know why God asked us to do something knowing we would never see it to completion. I don't understand why he invited us into a story and then let it hurt so bad. I don't know why God allowed this to happen with no given explanation around it. I don't understand why we were wounded as a result of our obedience. I don't know. I don't think I'll ever know this side of heaven.

I'm not sure why I went to Uganda. Years later and I'm still not sure if I'm honest. I don't know why I got to hold a little boy and tell him I loved him. I don't know what the point of all of that was. But this I know for sure, there is one little boy on the continent of Africa who rallied the troops and has had hundreds of people shaking the gates of heaven on his behalf for a long time now. People all over the globe praying for a little boy they will most likely never meet. There is something painfully beautiful about the whole thing.

I have learned that if we never open up our hearts, we will never get the chance to feel heartbroken. If we never love people, we will never get the chance to grieve them when they aren't with us anymore. If we never take a leap of faith, we never get to experience the crazy goodness of God in mid-air. If we never stand in a fire for God, we will never get to see him stand beside us in it. If we only ever live for Resurrection Sunday, we can never fully understand the sweetness of sitting in the darkness of Good Friday. If we only ever make safe, comfortable, predictable choices are we really doing what God has asked of us?

Life was teaching me that crap happens and it does not always come with a reason attached to it. Sometimes things happen for a reason, yes, other times things really don't happen for any reason at all. God was showing me he was big enough to wrestle with; he was willing to suit up, get on the mat and meet me where I was. He wasn't upset at me for being angry. He wasn't disappointed with my lack of faith. He wasn't bothered by my inability to trust him. He proved to be unshaken by my yelling and cursing and questions and demands for an explanation. Instead, he wrestled with me until I could wrestle no more. He blew the whistle signaling the match was over and raised his arm in the air declaring him to be the winner. He didn't celebrate or make me feel like the loser I knew I was; instead, he opened his arms wide and allowed me to collapse into them. He pulled me in for a hug and gently whispered to my heart *Child, I don't owe you anything.* He doles out limps and blessings. He's a good, good father.

I sat in church one morning and heard someone define the word "hallelujah" as commanding your soul to rejoice. Those words caught me off guard a little bit. They jolted me awake and breathed life back into my hurting soul. Those words felt like a salve to my broken, angry heart. That definition felt real and raw and the exact opposite of the fluffy Christian mess I couldn't stand anymore. Because contrary to popular belief sometimes life can throw you a serious curveball that knocks the breath out of you and kicks you to your knees. You could have believed in God your entire existence and find yourself questioning every last thing about him. Sometimes life hands you a deck of cards that leaves you feeling alone, hurt, tricked and fooled by that very same God you proclaimed to believe in. Sometimes you can find yourself not even sure you want to believe in him if this is how life is going to go down, and the last thing on planet Earth you want to do is rejoice and praise and say "Hallelujah." But it's easy to proclaim God's goodness in the light; the hard part is doing it in the dark. Sometimes when we are standing in the darkness, we can forget what has been promised to us in the light. Sometimes we must command our souls to rejoice. Sometimes we must offer up a broken hallelujah.

As if I were my own teacher I assigned myself some homework. I commanded myself to rejoice. I forced myself to praise God out loud for who he was and this is what I discovered; if I believe the Bible to be true, then I believe who it says God is and if I believe who God says he is then at some point I have to stop questioning who he says he is and simply accept it. I can either continue to throw down, or I can get up and accept that God is awesome, good, powerful, just, faithful, everlasting, sovereign, and perfect. He was those things the day we sat on our front porch and said yes to adoption. He was those things the day we saw JT's face and knew in our guts it was another yes. He was those things the day I stood in my house in Uganda and heard the words, "You can't adopt him anymore." He was those things then, and he is those things now. He will be those things the day we stand with our next child, and he will still be those things if we never hold a child. He is who he says he is yesterday and today and tomorrow and forever. He is who he says he is in the broken and the beautiful and the messy. He is who he says he is when we believe it easily, and more importantly he is who he says he is when we forget.

4

THE ONES WHO SHOULD HAVE BEEN

Dustin asked me what I wanted to do for Mother's Day weekend and I didn't know anything other than I didn't want to go to church. Sometimes church is not the place to go when you are hurting. If you've never experienced a church on Mother's Day, it is very nice. Sometimes people hand out flowers at the door or during the service. Other times they will ask all the mothers to stand as the congregation applauds them. I have sat in churches who decided to honor the women with a fellow woman speaker or a message centered on motherhood. A church we used to attend likes to create a cute backdrop where you can take pictures with your kids and families and then hashtag the mess out of it on social media.

But this year I couldn't stomach any of that. It felt a little too in my face. I wasn't sure I was strong enough to sit through or endure it all. I felt certain if left unattended I might fight someone. Everything was still tender; it was all too fresh for this. It's hard when you're trying to mend a wound, but the world wants to open it back up and make it bleed again. For the first time in my life, this day became complicated. What about the ones who should have been? What about us?

I should have been a mom right then. I should have been a real, physical mom to a toddler. I should have been called, "mommy." I should have been tucking him into bed every night and reading bedtime stories. I should have been taking him to the park and the zoo. I should have been teaching him how to ride that red bike. I should have been so tired because I was chasing a crazy three-year-old around all the live long day. I should have been watching *Curious George*, singing the ABC's, and teaching Bible stories.

I should have had funny stories of life with a toddler, and I should have also had tough stories of life with a toddler. I should have been able to laugh with other moms as we shared stories of raising little human beings. I should have been coordinating play dates and outings to the park.

I should have been having conversations with my husband about parenting. I should have been laughing with him over funny things our little boy did and said. I should have been getting babysitters so we could go on what parent's call "date night." I should have been forming family traditions and having family dinners. I should have been sending my husband and son off on boys' only outings.

I should have been celebrating Mother's Day for the first time that weekend. I should have been the one getting flowers at the door and applauded as I stood. I should have been the one getting a cute homemade card and going to brunch with my family. I should have been the one taking all the cute pictures. I should have been a mom right then, and I wasn't. And you know what? It burned like fire.

Because I was a mom, but I wasn't a mom. I could feel the tension so thick in my heart. I was a mom for a minute, but I didn't have anything to show for it. Nothing about this made any sense- I wasn't a mom, but I had been. I should have been. I couldn't shake it. I learned that year people don't celebrate things that should have been. They don't make should have been cards, and it's hard to post a picture of something that should have been but isn't. You cannot go to brunch with your should have been family. People are not recognized for things they should have been but in fact actually are not.

I desperately wanted to be seen but not pitied. I felt so furious when most people wouldn't utter his name out of their mouths as if they had suddenly forgotten it. I wanted to be able to say it out loud freely. I didn't want to be tiptoed around or treated like a giant elephant that was in the room. I wanted to be treated normally. I wanted to laugh, and I wanted the space to cry. I wanted to be remembered for who I was before everything hit the fan. I needed people to ask me questions and then be okay with the exact answers I gave. I didn't want to hear one person's opinion on the whole thing.

There were two people in Austin my heart really needed to see, and so we packed it up and headed out of town for the weekend. There was something incredibly healing about those days. Being with people who weren't afraid of what happened to me almost felt like holy ground. Those few days were filled with the ordinary stuff of life, and I hadn't had that in months. The last morning we were there, my friend Jamie and I went for a walk. We talked about a lot of things from marriage to church to friends to family to what happened. She asked me a question that led to one of my favorite conversations. She asked me, "How are you making sense of all of this?" No one had asked me that question yet, and it opened up a space I will forever be grateful for.

She listened as I talked it out. She listened as I told her I think this was all God's plan but how I also don't know if I believe in a God who would plan something like this. She listened as I talked through how I also think this was all Satan and how I believe God let Satan do it. She listened as I told her how I also don't know how to make sense of any of it and there are days I really don't care why it happened, it just sucks.

She didn't say anything. I honest to God don't think she uttered more than ten words. She never told me what she thought about what happened or how much it was affecting her. She didn't try to make my views on God pretty. She didn't try to make sense of or find closure for me in my pain. She didn't tie a pretty bow on my grief. She simply asked an excellent question and then let the conversation be messy. It is one of those moments I will carry with me forever.

I was learning that hurting people don't need you to make sense of their pain. When people tried to make sense of my pain, it hurt even more. I didn't need anyone to fix my grief for me because there was nothing to fix. I didn't need anyone to find closure in my pain. And every time someone would say to my face, "Everything happens for a reason" or "One day you'll understand why all of this happened" or something about "God's plan for our life" or "Maybe you just weren't ready to be a mom" that's what it felt like.

Not long after I returned home from Uganda, I reached out to a friend who has a similar story and asked, "How do you find closure in situations where there is no closure? Does it just haunt you forever?" I needed to know if I would ever function properly again or if this had eternally messed me up for good. She was so kind in her response. She simply said, "It gets better. You will never move on, and you will never forget. You will just be different. You will find a new normal. You will figure out a way to live here and have a piece of your heart missing. You will find a way to function and live and also remember. It will get better. You will get better." She was right; over time it did get better. Over time I got better.

I didn't know how lonely grief was until all of a sudden I did. I had forgotten how often we judge others for their grief until I was the one being judged for grieving something that didn't fit into a box. I may not have known what it was like to have a child die or have a miscarriage or to lose a parent or whatever the next reason someone was grieving, but I had walked away from a child I had prepared for and thought would be my son. I had physically walked away from him, and it had been crushing. We only know our own experiences, and we can only share our own truths. Grief is grief. A loss is a loss. It's all a freaking nightmare.

But gradually, over time, my grief began to soften. And then I attended my first baby shower, and I wanted to stab someone. I cannot explain the feelings of rage and jealousy and heartbreak I felt as I watched a friend open gifts for the little boy I didn't have. I went to the bathroom a lot during that party, and I took a lot of deep breathes in there. I sobbed the entire way home. Grief comes and goes in waves I was learning, and as soon as you think you're okay you walk through Target and see the same exact clothes other people bought for the kid who would never get to wear them, and suddenly you can't breathe anymore. I forced myself to hang out with friends for the longest time, and it was miserable. I pretended to laugh and smile, and it was all so fake. One night I went to dinner with friends who were all pregnant; I listened to them talk about everything baby and my feelings were so hurt. I ordered another beer and sat at the table and endured the conversation with gritted teeth, and then I cried the whole way home. It was all so devastating. I hated going places because people were weird around me. They didn't know if they should bring it up or pretend it didn't happen, and so I became someone who was tiptoed around, and I despised it. Pain is awkward. Still to this day, multiple calendar years later, some people refer to JT as "the first one," and I sincerely want to punch them in the face. He has a name, and you know it; say it. We're so afraid of other people's heartbreak. But then one day I hung out with friends and genuinely enjoyed it. I didn't force myself to go, and it felt like a huge deal because it was. I received an invitation to a baby shower, went and didn't hate it. I got in the car and cried about the fact that I didn't hate it but I had not wanted to murder everyone in the room that day, and it felt like odd progress. After believing I would never care about anything dumb ever again I found myself caring about The Bachelorette and I was kind of upset about it. Like, how can I care about this garbage while my heart is broken and I'm so sad, and the little boy I love will never be my son? It felt good and weird and sad.

Grief is so terrible. It ebbs, and it flows and it never really goes away. Some days it was big and overwhelming, and other days it wasn't. Sometimes grief felt like fire ants attacking me and other times it felt like a toothache. Some days I forgot about it. I was learning there is no way to be awesome at grief. You just do it and figure it all out as you go. I was learning that no two people grieve the same way. Dustin and I had to do this part separately, and that was okay. I was learning that hurting people will come to their own conclusions about what they experienced. They will make sense of it, they really will. It may take a long time, and it may be a different conclusion every other day, but they will do it, and they will do it for themselves. I was beginning to grasp that there is power in simply sitting quietly in someone else's pain with them while they worked it out. There is something good and holy about running towards someone's pain and asking how they are making sense of their experience and being okay with a messy answer. That right there is how healing started to happen.

And then out of nowhere, I felt God tell me it was time to let it all go but I didn't want to. Sharing a story with someone else was proving to be more difficult than I had initially expected it would be. We had always said we would not be sharing the story of our child with anyone; how he had come to be adoptable in the first place was not for anyone else to know. It wasn't anyone's business but his and ours. We agreed that if one day he chose to share his story with others that would be his decision and we would support that, but we would never share it for him. His story was never ours to tell. Then everything hit the fan, and his story still was not ours to tell, and it sucked. Protecting the details of a story that is not yours but that you are a part of is lonely.

I couldn't let it go. It felt wrong to. I was scared to. I thought if I let it go it meant I was okay with what happened and I wasn't. I figured if I let it all go it meant that I would forget. It turns out that isn't true. You don't ever truly move on, and you don't ever forget. You just become different. You find a new normal. You figure out a way to live here and have a piece of your heart missing. You find a way to function and live and also remember. It turns out letting things go is okay. But I didn't know that yet.

But that whisper: *Let it go. It's okay. You can set it down, in my name, and keep walking. I will take care of him. He is mine. He has always been mine. I called you by faith to start something, and you did. That is all I asked you to do. I've got him.*

I spent that summer wrestling with peace. I wrestled with it because I thought for a really long time that peace meant acceptance, as if feeling peace about him meant I approved it all. I thought feeling peace with what happened meant I had to sing it is well with my soul and mean it. But it wasn't well with my soul, and I don't think it ever will be. I don't know if it ever should be. There was something so final about being asked to feel peace; it felt like the door was closing on this story. I could feel in my bones something else was out there, something else was waiting for us, and I wasn't ready for it yet. It was like God was telling me I couldn't go there until peace found its way into my heart.

God and I suited up again; if he wanted me to feel peace than we were going to have to wrestle through this one, too. We had done it before. We spent some major time together. I yelled at him all over again. I cried as I prayed big prayers for a little voiceless human being who didn't ask for this story. I begged him to open doors and move on behalf of one little boy. I tried to explain that if he would just make something happen, anything, we would tell the story and it would reek of Jesus. I scoured through the book of Isaiah and read about how God is a God of justice. I read the words that tell us how he desperately cares about the lost. How his heart is for the orphan and the oppressed, and I pushed back. I questioned who he was again because we were a part of something that didn't seem just. This whole thing felt like the exact opposite of caring for the orphan.

But that whisper told me otherwise. It was real, and it was constant, like God was chanting in my ear: *I've got him. He is mine. I will protect him. He is loved. He is wanted. He is my son. I will take care of him. I will be the one who sees this to completion. You are a part of something that only I will finish. Keep walking by faith.*

That summer we were living in a season where it felt like everyone and their dog was either having a baby, trying to have a baby, talking about trying to have a baby, or bringing their newly adopted baby home from wherever. These seasons come and go in waves it feels like. Sometimes no one is pregnant, and sometimes everyone is. Sometimes new life is everywhere we go, and other times it simply isn't. It's so fun to be surprised by friends as they tell you they're pregnant. Walking with friends as they adopt a child and then meeting them for the first is the best. Celebrating with your people is a sweet thing; it's always sweet.

And in the midst of all that sweetness, it felt really bitter, too. Wanting a family and not having one yet was hard. It was just hard; that's all. Watching other people get what you should already have sucked. Sometimes life is bittersweet. I spent a lot of time that summer ugly crying in the name of celebration, good things, and exciting news. I ugly cried in my car, in the shower, under my covers, openly at my kitchen table, and in many a bathroom stall. I ugly cried in church on Father's Day when the preacher asked all the dads to stand, and my husband remained seated. I had a thing for a while where I would ugly cry while running and for the record doing both is somewhat challenging. It's kind of like sneezing while brushing your teeth; it's not impossible, but it's also not attractive. Bittersweet cries are a strange breed of cries.

But God was beckoning me to lay down my grief not forget about it. He was asking me to hold on to the crappy pieces of our story while recognizing it also wasn't finished yet. He was inviting me out of the trenches of grief by way of a bittersweet life. God was granting me permission to hurt and keep living. That summer I turned the corner. I claimed the word bittersweet as my own and God breathed new life into my hurting soul. It became my anthem, and I wasn't afraid to use it. It felt like rubbing a salve on my freshly battered heart. There was something extremely holy about not being afraid to hold space for the tension of life. I was learning that loss, grief, joy, celebrations, and wanting but not having yet could all coexist in the same space. I found Jesus right there in the midst of it all.

I became extremely aware of how often we cling to silver linings and happy endings. How desperate we are to fix pain rather than feel it. We are so not okay with life being messy. We want answers and for things to make sense and we want those things now. We are not very good at living in or allowing others to live in tension; especially within the context of faith. But Jesus ran towards people's pain, and when I did the same I found freedom where freedom is always found; in the truth and it set me free all over again. Sometimes life is really sweet, and sometimes it really isn't. Other times it's both, and that's completely okay.

I can't tell you exactly how it happened, but all I know is eventually that whisper won me over. Very slowly that whisper became louder in my heart than all of the details on paper. Over time that whisper redefined for me the words used to describe that little boy. I still wanted big things for him. I still prayed bold, mighty prayers on behalf of him. Nothing about anything made sense to me. I wasn't sure if it would ever not hurt to think about him. But I did know that God was good, and he was beckoning me out of the darkness to come into the light. He was inviting me to feel peace even though it didn't make sense to. He was asking me to trust him again. He was inviting me to experience redemption. He was about to show me for the first time but not the last that beauty can rise from ashes if we allow them to.

5

BEAUTIFUL TORTURE

I woke up one more morning feeling like it was time. I wasn't ready, but it needed to be done. I poured a cup of coffee, turned on Justin Timberlake and opened up the door to JT's room. I walked over and sat on his bed. It had striped sheets with a blue comforter on it. There was a Mater, from the movie *Cars*, pillow sitting on his bed one of my sisters had bought for him. The walls were blue; I remember standing in the paint aisle carefully choosing a shade of blue just for him. I had stayed up late every night for a week painting those walls. His dresser was full of the cutest little boy clothes I couldn't wait for him to wear. A giraffe was sitting on top of the dresser next to his lamp. The rocking chair sat by the door next to a basket of books. I had imagined bedtime stories and rocking that sweet boy to sleep. There was a rug on the floor that had car tracks drawn on it with a basket of cars sitting beside it. I had dreamed of walking into his room to see him rolling cars on it.

I took the sheets off the bed, folded them up and put them in the closet. I put a pair of grey sheets on and laid a white comforter down on top of the bed. I boxed up books, puzzles, stuffed animals, and toys. I carefully folded every item of clothing and boxed them up by size. I took the picture of the elephant hanging on the wall over his bed down and replaced it with a painting of a flower. I turned that room we had created for JT back into a room we had originally created for guests. I loaded up my car, drove over to my parents' house and unloaded everything into their garage. The basketball goal, the t-ball set, and the red tricycle sat crammed in the back corner. I drove back home and entered a different house. The home that had been prepped for a little boy was no longer that. If a stranger had entered that afternoon, they wouldn't have had a clue. There is something incredibly painful about creating space in your home for a child who will never occupy it.

A few weeks later, I received an email from one of our social workers with pictures of two different children who needed a family; I sat on my couch shaking. I looked at their pictures, I read their stories, I wept, and I went to the bathroom, and dry heaved over the toilet. *Can I do this again? I'm still so sad. Am I brave enough to go back? I'm so scared. What if the same thing happens again? I might physically die. Can I love another kid like I loved JT? I'm terrified to.* For a month, I sat silently on those two pictures. I went back and forth. I couldn't decide if I wanted to go back. I didn't know if I wanted to it again. I didn't have to. I knew going back was the right thing to do, but you don't always have to do what is right. In the end, it was my husband; Dustin said the yes because I was too scared to. Without a word to another soul, we began again. We were going to have another son.

A really good friend asked me randomly if we had any adoption news we wanted to share. She said that if we didn't, for us to know they were still praying for our family. For the first time, I uttered, "Things are happening, but we're just waiting and not saying a whole lot." She proceeded to say the following, "Totally get that. When you are ready we want to hear, but not until then. I can't even imagine the beautiful torture of deciding to expose your hearts again."

I so desperately didn't want this to be our story. I wanted it to be someone else's, and I wanted to feel sad for them. I didn't want it to be mine. I didn't want to have to live it, carry it and I most certainly didn't want to have to tell it. But it was our story; it was the only one we knew, and it was the only story we had to tell. We started staking claims. I paced our house praying and proclaiming scriptures out loud. I declared hope over my heart. I claimed peace as my own. I pronounced trust where fear had snaked its way in. When anxiety hit me like an ocean wave, I vomited in the toilet and continued pacing. I commanded my soul to believe in who God says he is. Courage became my captor. We became prisoners to the fact that this story wasn't over yet, it was just beginning again, and we waited to go back.

I told some friends how fearful I was to go back to Uganda one day. How afraid I was to willingly get on a plane and fly myself back to the place where all of the hard things went down. How I was so scared I would get there and be paralyzed, paralyzed with sadness and fear and grief and anxiety. How genuinely terrified I was to do that again. One of them looked at me and said, "Courtney, do you remember how hard it was for you to come home? Going back is going to be really hard, but to me, you've already done the hardest thing." Another one said something to the tune of, "Yeah I wish we had video footage of you when you first came home so you could see yourself. You were in a really dark place." And then we had a good laugh.

I never thought about how hard it was to come home from Uganda. How physically sick I got when I received that phone call. How it seemed impossible to put on a smiling face and play with a little boy for the very last time. How devastating those plane rides home were. How sad it was to send that email telling everyone what happened. How cruel it felt to realize life keeps moving forward, it doesn't stop just because sad things happen. How horrible going back to work was. How sad and angry and hurt I was. How genuinely hard it was to do the work of grieving, and then how genuinely hard it was to do the work of healing and moving forward.

I get why we do it. I think part of it is protective. We don't look back because it hurts and it's hard, and it isn't fun. We don't think back because we're surviving and then when we aren't surviving we're figuring out a new normal. Moving forward makes it hard to remember sometimes. I think when hard things happen it's easy to forget where we started. When we're living in the aftermath of the hard, we aren't thinking about where we came from. But I was learning that if we never look back, it's impossible to see how far we've come.

I became really into the definition of courage those days: strength in the face of pain or grief. I was coming to believe that just like grief; courage did not belong in a box. While you can define what courage is you cannot define precisely what courage looks like. Courage is grieving; grieving the child you lost, the relationship you were hurt in, or the dream that died. Courage is surviving; getting up and making yourself eat and shower and get dressed. Courage is moving forward; finding new happiness in the midst of pain. Courage is looking back and remembering; remembering how hard it was and how okay you are now. Courage is doing tough things; packing up a room, going back to the place you were hurt, or talking about what happened. Courage: strength in the face of pain or grief. Yes, a thousand times yes.

I bought myself a necklace with the word courage on it and I wore it almost daily simply as a reminder. It wasn't so much a reminder to have courage but a reminder that I already did have it. I wanted it to say something like, "Girl, you can do hard $#*!" but apparently that's too long to get engraved on a necklace, and Dustin said something about that being inappropriate. To that I say, whatever, sometimes courage is inappropriate. I was learning that sometimes we need a reminder. We need someone to ask us, "Do you remember how hard it was for you to come home?" We need someone to tell us that you can do hard things. You've already done them.

6

HOPE

Will you still love me if the same thing happens again?
Will you still believe in me if you never adopt a child?

I remember when these questions started popping up in my heart. They caught me off guard at first. The more they popped up, the more they felt rude; intrusive almost. I'm not answering that. How dare you ask me that right now? I don't owe you an answer to that question. So I didn't give one. I carried on with my day pretending they weren't following me around demanding to be answered.

A lot of people were telling me that one day our story would be beautiful. I knew exactly what they meant, and I agreed. If we ever successfully adopted a child our story would be beautiful in a way I couldn't fully fathom yet. That sentence was hard though because I thought our story was already beautiful in a weird and broken way. It wasn't beautiful in a way that made sense or beautiful like a J Crew model. It was beautiful in a, "I shattered this plate because I was pissed that something crappy happened and then I decided to put it back together, but I'm missing a piece of it so this plate has got a really great story," kind of way.

Even though I thought I'd never arrive at acceptance one day I found myself there. Something terrible had happened, and our story was beautiful. It was beautiful just as it was, whether we added one hundred adopted children to our family or none. Our story was enough; nothing needed to be added to it to make it more enough or more beautiful. This story of ours was just that, our story. It was the only one we knew. It was the only one we had to tell. It was the only one we had to live. And so I found myself sitting in this place of pure and genuine acceptance; it felt like fresh air in my lungs. A holy peace came alongside that acceptance in a way I had not known. I knew it was holy because it didn't make sense; it passed every bit of my understanding. I had a holy peace that it had been right to pursue JT and it had been right to walk away. I had a holy peace going back was the right thing to do. Regardless of the outcome, whether I ever had a Ugandan residing under my roof or not, this was right. I found myself back at those questions but this time with a solid answer, yes.

I came home one afternoon and found a small surprise on my front porch for the tiny person we were not talking about but had vaguely mentioned maybe one time. I cried when I opened it and I cried when I saw who it was from. When I sent them a thank you I got this in response, "It can be very hard to plan for your next child after you lose the first one. In my case the first two. Thought I'd plan for you with this." I had a big, fat, weepy cry over the whole thing. The gift itself is not the thing that made me cry. While it was extremely nice and entirely unnecessary, the thing that made me cry was what the gift symbolized, hope. That tiny box on my front porch meant someone was hoping on our behalf. They were standing in the gap and doing the thing we couldn't do ourselves. They were hoping for us.

Hoping can be hard because hoping is just that, hope. It's the place we go to expect and anticipate and desire and want. It's the place we go to wait. It's the place we go knowing there are no guarantees. It's the place we go knowing everything may happen or nothing may happen. It's the place we go knowing we're just hoping.

Here's the thing about hope, it's vulnerable and raw. Hoping is brave, and it's courageous. Hoping is risky. Hoping is scary as all get out. Hoping is borderline terrifying. When you're staring hope right in the face hoping can feel insane. To hope after you've been hurt is ludicrous. To hope in the midst of the not yet is dangerous. To hope knowing the result may be the exact opposite of what you were hoping for in the first place is heavy stuff. But I was finding Jesus in the middle of all the hoping. I was also finding yoga and essential oils and my counselor, lest you think I'm all high and mighty. There is something about asking boldly and waiting expectantly after you've been hurt that can change a person. You just might find yourself believing deep within your soul that if not God is in fact still good.

I started proclaiming hope over my heart. I decided to straddle the line of asking and waiting expectantly and knowing full well God may say no or not yet again. I was choosing to hope because while other people can hope on your behalf, not one person can make you do it. I was telling myself over and over again the he was good, regardless of circumstances and regardless of outcomes. It was weird, and a part of me would have rather stayed guarded than to risk hope but to hope in Jesus is to hope in the not yet. To hope in the name of Jesus is holy ground.

Hope can rise out of ashes. Hallelujahs can be commanded of your soul. God can meet you right there on the wrestling mat in the midst of fear, uncertainty, and grief and prove to you exactly who he says he is. God is not only found on the mountain tops, but he is also walking right alongside us in ruins whispering, "I know you are hurt. I know you are scared. I know you are afraid to hope. I am right here. You can trust me when you're ready."

7

GOING BACK

When I first read JT's story chills covered my body and a giant lump formed in my throat. The same month he found himself in need of a family was the same month I felt so burdened to begin the adoption process. I don't think for one second that was a coincidence. If God can part an entire sea so people could cross it why could he not burden two people on behalf of a little boy a zillion miles away? I believe that was purposed. I will go to my grave believing we were always supposed to pursue him. I will also go to my grave firmly believing we were always supposed to walk away, too. But we were supposed to go; we always were.

A few months later the tiniest eighteen-month-old little boy I'd ever seen would hit my inbox. I sat on my couch reading his story through tears because I knew, yet again, it wasn't a coincidence. As we were praying all those prayers a year earlier this little boy's mom was doing exactly what we were praying for. As we were feeling burdened to adopt, his mom was in the late stages of pregnancy. While we were begging God to keep her and her baby safe, he did. As we were asking God to go before her and be in the delivery, he was. While we were praying prayers for life to be chosen, God chose it for him. As we were feeling overwhelmed with a sense of urgency, God was saying, yes but not yet. I have something else for you first and then, yes. We could have said no. We really could have. But, oh my word, I'm glad we didn't.

My dad pulled up to our house that morning in November, and we loaded our luggage into the bed of his red truck. I could barely look at him without a lump forming in the back of my throat. I felt ill; I was so scared. I had Dustin with me this time, but he would be coming back home in two weeks while I was headed out indefinitely, not sure when I'd be back or whether I'd have anyone with me upon my return this time. We drove silently to the airport; the air felt thick, the only noise was the radio. Everyone was anxious. I'm pretty sure I didn't even make eye contact with my dad as he hugged me goodbye. I couldn't. This trip was a secret; I couldn't invite the world in on this one, not again. I had to do this one on my own terms and in my own way. I owed myself that much. The heart can only risk so much. So we secretly left the country and headed back to Uganda.

When people heard we were going to continue pursuing adoption after JT they would say things like, "Oh I hope you don't adopt a little boy this time. It would be like you were trying to replace JT." But we were going back for a little boy who was never made to replace JT, and it was the hardest and most right thing we have ever done.

Before I left, I got a tattoo on my forearm. It has an outline of Africa and above it says "by faith." It was so symbolic for me. By faith, I walked away from JT because it was the right thing to do and by faith, I was going back because it was also the right thing to do. I have learned sometimes things that are right can also be the most painful. Sometimes joy comes at a cost.

Hebrews eleven is often called "The Hall of Faith." For several verses, it lists different men and women throughout the Bible who acted courageously by faith. They responded by faith to something the Lord asked of them regardless of the outcome. There was no game plan or steps one, two and three given ahead of time; instead they obediently acted simply by faith. And I had come to learn that acting by faith was not a simple task. I marveled at these men and women who just took the first step they were asked to take and let God take it from there. Sometimes all we've got to do is put one foot in front of the other. Going back to Uganda for me was an act of faith. It was taking the next step in obedience even though I had no clue how it was going to end. It was an act of courage. It was me confirming I believed in God and his goodness regardless of what happened next. It felt scary, and it also felt right.

We woke up a few mornings later, crawled out of the mosquito net which was wrapped around the bed and silently ate breakfast. Our driver knocked on the door and ushered us to his car. I stared out the window the entire two-hour ride to the orphanage. I watched as the city turned into beautiful, green hills. My whole body shook as we made our way off of paved roads and onto red dirt roads. My heart pounded as I tried to convince myself I could do this internally. I could meet another child who was supposed to be my son. I could love again.

As we pulled up to the orphanage I leaned over to Dustin, tears in my eyes and almost choked out, "You're going to have to do this. I don't think I can. I don't think I can hold him. You're going to have to do this." Dustin looked me dead in the eyes and said, "Ok. I'll do it." I looked out the window at the buildings in front of me; one of those rooms housed my son. I watched all the kids running around knowing they knew him. I saw babies being carried and I wondered which one was him. I took a deep breath, got out of the car and was immediately greeted by swarms of children with giant smiles and big eyes, all wanting hugs and for us to play with them. We were walked back to a small, hot office where we waited.

As we sat in that room talking and waiting for one of the sweet caregivers to bring him to us, I thought, *I'm going to puke. I don't know any of these people, and I'm going to throw up on all of them. This is going to be so awkward. Do I offer to clean it up? Do I pretend I'm actually sick and not scared out of my mind? I cannot do this. I can't. What was I thinking? This is a load of crap. I was an idiot to think I could come back and do this again. I hate this. Would it be weird to walk out?*

I will never forget watching a woman walking towards me carrying the tiniest, most beautiful one and a half year old I'd ever seen. He was so small and so striking. Someone said, "This is

Mukisa" as she handed him straight to me. I froze. I paused. I will never get over the fact that I hesitated before reaching out my arms to hold my son.

The second he was in my arms he screamed one of the saddest, most terrified screams I have ever heard in my entire life. His eyes were huge, and they were scared. If he could have jumped out of my arms, I think he would have. If I could have handed him off without it being awkward, I think I would have. It was not the moment I envisioned or even wanted it to be but looking back it was perfect. Two terrified strangers who would eventually become a family meeting for the first time. What else would you expect? All I remember is looking at him and thinking, "I'm so scared too, buddy. I'm going to love you. We're going to be okay. We are. But I'm scared, too."

I stood outside my house in Uganda waiting for my driver to come to pick me up for court a few weeks later. The judge would not wait if I were late. Dustin had gone home, and I was alone. This was it. I had studied the facts of our case and knew the details like I knew the back of my hand. I had prepared answers for questions that might be asked. I was as ready as you can be. I paced my house half sobbing, half calm as a cucumber patiently waiting. My driver arrived very late because if you've ever heard of "Africa Time" that is very much a thing. We sped through the streets of Uganda while I sat in the front seat begging God for mercy and trying not to get car sick. My lawyer called multiple times demanding I be at the courthouse. I jumped out of the moving vehicle, running into the courthouse where I met my social worker, witnesses, and our disgruntled lawyer. He pleaded with the judge to see our case in light of the time, and she eventually agreed to. I nervously walked back to the judge's chambers, Mukisa already trying to squirm his way out of my arms and sat down in front of the judge. The air was impenetrable, serious; a child's future was in the hands of this room.

For two hours I sat and listened to testimonies being given in a language I could not understand. I watched the judge shake her head at answers being given, panic rising in my chest each time. I heard her ask questions in loud, cynical ways and it didn't feel good. When you don't understand the language being spoken you have no clue how anything is going and so I sat, prayed and wrangled the toddler in the room. Each time he screamed or jumped off the chair or crawled under her desk or messed with something or threw his bottle at someone's face or attempted to crawl out of the room the judge glared at me like I was the mom I didn't feel like I was. Then it was my turn. I stood up, raised my right hand and swore I would tell the truth. I begged the window beside me to shut on its own as the sound of city traffic became louder than the whisper of the questions being asked of me. I prayed the Holy Lord would overcome my child with a bout of sleepy-ness he could not fight. I sweated through my shirt as I was drilled with questions- Why are you so young? Can you even care for a child at your age? How can I believe you? How will you be a mom? What will you do when he cries? How will you discipline? What will you teach him about Uganda? What do you know about his particular tribe? What does his name mean? I stumbled through answers, cussing in my head, bouncing up and down this child I didn't know yet on my hip. I didn't even know if he liked to be bounced on the hip. I told the judge we would love him, take care of him, provide for him, and take pride in every part of him. I sat back down, closed my eyes, exhaled, and prayed; prayed that only if this was right would it happen. A week later that judge said we could do it; we could be his parents.

I would end up spending nine and a half weeks off the grid in Uganda. Dustin was there for the first two of those weeks; my parents came to stay with me for several days, but most of those weeks I was by myself. I did my laundry by hand and hung clothes on the clothesline to dry. I went grocery shopping and figured out how to cook without any of my regular American staples. I went out to eat when I needed something that resembled American food and always had a fun time in the bathroom afterward. I threw up out the window of our moving vehicle one time because sometimes life is just too much to handle. My driver, Eddie, who is now one of my most favorite humans on planet earth stood beside me patting my back as I heaved outside of his car. I figured out the ins and outs of living with unreliable electricity. I went to church on Sundays. The days were slow and the nights were long. It was a sweet time that also felt nerve-wracking, unbearably lonely and boring. I wanted to go home more days than I did not.

I became a mom overnight to a scared and grieving eighteen-month-old in another country all by myself. Sometimes the weight of that catches me off guard. I did a passport interview outside under a tent in the hot Ugandan sun. I wrestled a baby through doctor's appointments and embassy interviews. I had no chill the day the guards outside of the U.S. Embassy told me I could not bring in a bottle for my child who cried exactly always. "How am I supposed to answer questions in there with a screaming baby? Are you coming inside to help me?" I yelled. "Drink the milk, so we know there is nothing in there" they responded. I have never chugged formula milk so hard in all of my life. I lost my mind on government officials and became a private investigator trying to figure out what in the world was happening with our case when nothing was moving forward.

I got my first real taste of what grief in a baby can look like. I learned that grief could not be tamed; as I had experienced earlier grief must be lived through, toddlers are no exception. I rocked an inconsolable screaming baby boy for weeks on end both day and night. I changed diapers, and I sang songs. I played peek-a-boo and read books and rolled cars back and forth endlessly. I watched that little boy learn to laugh and begin to trust skeptically. The two of us never slept. I taught him to walk regardless of what my dad has to say about it. I learned how to be a mom in that country. Then just like that, we were out of there doing something like twenty hours of travel; me and my son Wyatt Mukisa. Mukisa means "blessing" or "luck" in Uganda, and while I don't know if I believe in luck I do believe in blessings, and that sweet boy sure has grown into one of the greatest blessings of my entire life. On January 25th, 2015 we became a family of three stateside. It was a thrill to introduce our long-awaited son to the world.

Sometimes life has seasons that are simply meant to be lived in real time. I could never go back and speak about those days well. It feels almost intensely private. Wyatt and I have experienced things together no one else will ever experience with us. Those days were overwhelming, and they were gritty. We were just two scared strangers awkwardly attempting to figure out this whole mother/son dance.

Adoption is always so many different things and that day we landed in America was no different. It felt big, real and final. I was overwhelmed at the thought of all my little boy had lost in his short not quite yet two years of life. I looked at him in awe of all he had already overcome. I marveled at the fact that this was not perfect, this was not God's original plan for a child, but it was good. He was rising up something beautiful from ashes. He was breathing life back into a little soul that was crushed. He was breathing life back into my own soul that had been smashed. He was about to turn a motley crew of strangers into a family. Won't he do it? I held onto that little boy, my little boy, and I thanked God for him. A family lost, and a family gained. This is adoption.

What I didn't know then is that I would fall hard for that little boy. When I wasn't sure if my heart could love again he would show me that it could. That tiny baby boy taught me that it's okay to go scared. He did it. My son joined our family terrified. I will honor that until the day I die. I was beginning to understand that just because you're scared doesn't mean you're doing anything wrong. I can now proclaim from the rooftops that sometimes something will never not be scary, and you will just have to do the thing afraid.

If I could go back and tell myself anything it would be this: *Hang on, sister. That boy you are so afraid to love is going to steal your heart in every way. It's going to take a long, long time and it's not going to be easy. He is going to grieve by never sleeping and screaming bloody murder for most of a year. You will not always handle that well. Buy some earplugs and don't take it personally. Take my advice now because you do not do these things. Trust me he will not have parasites forever. Let your mom babysit him. He will cry, and he will also be fine, and you will be better because of it. You will wonder if he will ever like you. You will wonder if you will ever like him. You are going to mess up. You are going to doubt yourself. You will cry. You will yell. Give him grace. Give yourself more. You will feel like a babysitter for so long. One day you won't. He will one day stop crying. He will one day be happy. You will be scared to say anything about it for fear of jinxing it, but it's real. You can go ahead and celebrate. He's really, really happy.*

One day you will fall madly in love with him, and it will be everything you ever wanted it to be. He's going to fall in love with you, too. This thing that felt so forced for so long will one day feel so natural it will overwhelm you. You will feel fiercely protective of him. The two of you will become the best of friends. He's going to make you laugh so hard. People are going to tell you to enjoy every moment. You will want to punch them. You won't and you shouldn't. You also will not enjoy every moment and you shouldn't. Not every moment is meant to be enjoyed. One day you will miss him, though. You will be sad when he starts preschool because you're going to miss him. You believe deep down that he will change the world and simultaneously the thought of sending him to kindergarten will make you want to keep him forever. I know it's hard to imagine now, but you're going to miss him one day.

He's going to call you his best girl so much that one day when he tells you he has another best girl you are going to feel a rage you did not know existed within you. He is going to wake up every morning and crawl in bed with you and whisper, "Excuse me, mommy? Can I snuggle with you?" You're going to snuggle with him so hard and be so sad when it's over. That boy you were so afraid to love will one day feel like a distant memory. Just wait for it.

8

BEING READY

For five out of the nine and half weeks I was in Uganda I visited Wyatt before he was legally allowed to leave his orphanage and come live with me. For five weeks I drove two hours there, stayed a few hours, and drove two hours back to the city where I was staying. I loved going to visit him because I got to see him. I got to know him, on his turf, and in his environment. I taught him to roll cars back and forth and play peek-a-boo. I got to hold him and sing to him and rock him to sleep. I hated going to visit him because I had to leave him. I had to walk away from a child I was trying to form a relationship with, a child I was supposed to view as my own, but was waiting for someone else to tell me whether this was or wasn't going to happen. I was asking a child to trust me, to risk love, and then every single time I walked away. Those visits were both sweet and rotten.

The screams that occurred when I left, make me sick to my stomach to think about still to this day. There is something so unnatural, almost out- of- body, about having to walk away from a screaming baby, a baby who is screaming specifically for you. A baby who is screaming for you to stay and then will scream all over again for months because you took him away. Grief is puzzling like that. When it was time to go, I would hand him back to one of his caregivers and walk away. I would turn around and march back to my car never once looking back; I couldn't look back, with a giant lump in my throat, thinking this had to be the world's worst plan. How can this, what I am currently doing, be good for a kid? As I would walk, listening to the howls of the baby who is now my own, I would say over and over and over again: "Please God let him be okay. Please God let him be okay. Please God let him be okay." All the way back to the car, and the two hours back to the city, I had those words on repeat.

One of my favorite things to do while I was visiting Wyatt was to sing him songs and rock him to sleep. One day I showed up, and a little girl walked up to me and said, "He cries when you are not here, and he sings your songs." Bless. And so day after day I would rock that boy and sing him my songs and hold him while he slept. When I thought he was finally deep in sleep, I would stop moving, stop singing, very slowly attempt to sit down and start praying. Those days in Uganda taught me that prayers don't need to be pretty or wordy or strung together beautifully; God hears the deepest moans of our hearts. The only two words I could muster out those days were, please God. I said those words over and over again while my boy slept in my arms.

Please God, let this happen. Please God, let me be okay if it doesn't. Please God, let this be ethical. Please God, let this be honorable. Please God, keep Satan away. Please God, make me believe regardless of the outcome. Please, God. Please, God. Please, God.

One day not long after we were home, in America, I was rocking Wyatt and holding him while he slept. I hadn't done that much since the Uganda days, but for whatever reason, I sat in the rocking chair beside his bed rocking that little boy back to sleep. I held him the way he liked to be held, and I rocked him just the right way, and as his eyelids closed and his breathing settled in I found myself back in Uganda sitting in the shade rocking a baby I didn't know and only longed to call my son. As I sat there in the dark with the little boy I was still getting to know I found myself grateful. As he twitched and drooled and turned his head over exhaling, all things I was still memorizing about him, I remembered the days my soul could only beg God for mercy.

I was so scared to love him. I was deathly afraid of falling in love with him only to have to walk away again. I was so guarded; I put the idea of love in my back pocket as something I would reach for later only if I ever became a mother. I was so afraid I'd hurt him as I had done to another little boy residing on the same continent. I was unconvinced he would ever be my son. I did not believe we would ever board an airplane and walk through the doors of our home together.

Going back to Uganda was solely an act of faith, and as I sat there rocking; I was reminded of how much I had to reconcile within the walls of my heart as it pertained to my faith. How hard it was to arrive at the place of believing, genuinely believing with my entire being, God was still good even if the same thing happened again. I looked down at that tiny, sleeping baby boy of mine and felt overwhelmed with gratitude. He was growing and changing. He was growing and changing us, too. We still had so much to learn about each other, but we were doing it. We were slowly but surely turning ourselves into the family I was unsure we'd ever be. This time I exhaled a thank you, God. How sweet it is to find life at the end of a long, dark tunnel. What a gift.

Dustin and I only bought one thing for Wyatt before I left for Uganda. It was too hard to prepare again for something that might never happen. I boarded an airplane with a bag full of items other people purchased for our child. We did not do one thing to prepare our home for his potential arrival. I couldn't do it, not this time. As I was leaving Uganda, baby in tow, I found myself frantically emailing Dustin things like, *we need onesies! And a highchair! A bed and sheets! Diapers! I think we're supposed to put things in the electrical outlets!! AND OH MY GOD WE NEED A PEDIATRICIAN!!!* He ran all over creation prepping our house for the baby I was too afraid to plan for. But we did buy the one thing, though. A few weeks before we left the country we were roaming around an African festival not far from our house. I found myself staring at all the baby clothes too afraid to touch them. Before we left, I was overcome with the feeling that we needed to·buy something. I looked at a rack of tiny dashikis and thought, "We should buy this for the child I don't think will ever come home with us." So we did.

A year later as we were getting ready for church I pulled that dashiki out of the back of the closet and put it on that dream of a baby boy now a toddler wreaking havoc inside the home I didn't believe he'd ever live in. We let him loose in the front yard, and as I stood on the front porch for a quiet minute, I was overwhelmed with the thought of missing this. *Remember that time you never thought he'd ever be here? Remember how much that hurt? Remember how much you wanted this and how afraid you were to do it again? Remember how you said no? Remember when your husband said yes? Remember how scary that was?*

A friend asked me once how I got to the place of being ready to adopt again after a loss, and I almost laughed in her face because I didn't. I wasn't ready, and I don't think I ever would have been ready. But sometimes the thing you're supposed to do is also the thing you'll never be ready to do, and if you wait to be ready, you just might miss it all together.

9

CHOOSING LOVE

Fighting for love is something I never expected I'd have to do as a mother. Sure, I knew there would be moments I might not particularly like my child but feel warm, fuzzy, genuine love for them? Not on the list. No one talks about this, this shameful secret of having to grow to love your child. It feels dirty almost to say out loud. People would look at us from the outside and think sweet, precious thoughts about our family but they didn't know the truth. Nobody wants to know this truth; the reality that we were forging through the awkward waters of falling in love with each other.

Being handed a stranger who speaks a different language to care for is just that, being given a stranger who speaks a different language to care for. I didn't know him. I didn't know whether he liked to be rocked or held or bounced or if he would rather me stand and sway while he was upset. I didn't know if he wanted me to rub his back or leave him alone while he tried to fall asleep. I didn't know what he liked to eat. I didn't know what made him laugh and I didn't know what made him mad. I didn't know his cry, not yet. I couldn't have picked it out of a room of crying babies. It didn't feel natural; it didn't feel like second nature being a mom. And it's easy when nothing feels right, and you don't know someone you're taking care of to take every last thing personally because nothing was right. He hated everything I did. I grew to feel paralyzed in parenting him. I thought maybe I wasn't the right mom for him. Maybe this was a mistake? Why can't I figure this out? Why don't I feel love? Am I a monster?

But here's the thing I didn't understand then, Wyatt didn't love me at first either. It looked like he might have from the outside, but sometimes survival can look like love. Just like I didn't know him, he didn't know me either. He didn't know my face or my eyes or my smile. He didn't know my voice or the sound of my laugh. He didn't know the way his little body would fit against mine. He didn't know if I was going to feed him when he was hungry or pick him up when he cried. He wasn't sure anyone would come running when he screamed in the night. He didn't trust me, not yet. And why would he? I had been the person who had taken him away from everything he had ever known.

People always want to know what it was like to meet Wyatt and JT for the first time. My answer is always the same, it was bizarre. They brought JT in and told him I was his new mom. They brought Wyatt in, and he screamed terrified screams the second they handed him to me. People are staring at you, watching everything you do. It was awkward and weird and not this precious, amazing thing. I didn't feel anything, other than like I was going to throw up both times. I didn't just know I was supposed to be either of their moms. I didn't feel different meeting Wyatt than I did meeting JT. I didn't feel overcome with mom feelings or heart eyes or go mushy with love feelings. I just didn't. I know people who have had that experience, and I think it's fantastic and extraordinary. Instead, both times, I looked at precious Ugandan faces, and I said in my head: "I will love you. I choose to love you."

I whispered, "I love you" to Wyatt day after day, month after month begging God to let me feel it. It felt fake, awkward, this dance of falling in love with my son. I sat at our kitchen table one night and through tears asked Dustin, "Do you feel it? Do you love him? Do you feel like a dad? How do you know?" But sometimes falling in love requires grit. Sometimes it demands determination. Sometimes it necessitates a march, a fight. I don't know if you've ever had to fight for love in this way, but I fought for Wyatt. We fought for each other; we fought like hell for love.

Adoption was teaching me that love is a choice. We like to talk about love as if it's a feeling but love is a verb, too. I was learning that I can choose love whether or not I feel love. It reminded me of marriage in some ways. Whether I want to or not, whether I feel anything or not, I can always choose to love- to be kind, patient, to care for, and be selfless. Love is not something I will always feel, and that is okay. But I can choose to love without feeling love because love is an action word. Love is not always an easy choice, and it doesn't always make sense. Choosing love is not always accompanied with heart eyes and tingly feelings. Choosing to love doesn't always mean you will feel love just because you chose it.

Adoption was teaching me that love is also a feeling. You can choose to love without feeling love, and then one day you can feel actual love. Love as a feeling doesn't always happen immediately. Love as a feeling is something that is living; it grows and evolves as the relationship changes. I didn't know it was okay to have to fall in love with your child just as I had to fall in love with my husband. But then one day it happened. I felt it. I honest to God fell in love with that boy. I loved him so much it hurt. It was like all the other moms I knew talked about freely; this love they had for their child that physically hurt sometimes. One night before bed he ran into our kitchen, wrapped his squishy little arms around my legs and for the first time unprompted said, "Love you, mommy." We did it. We fought for love, and we won.

A lot of people say in regards to adoption they aren't sure they could ever love a child who they did not birth biologically. I get it. But sometimes love is a choice first and a feeling second. Don't let the world tell you otherwise. Love takes work; it requires perseverance. That's what becoming a mom overnight to a grieving child I didn't know taught me. Choosing to love is a powerful choice, and we can always choose to love.

Wyatt is one of the bravest people I know. He didn't choose this story; people don't like to think about that. He didn't choose the life he was handed. I feel confident one day we will all walk the fine line with him of loving his life and wishing it had happened differently. Maybe we won't but one day we might. Instead, this life was handed to him, and he overcame it. He's a survivor, a fighter.

The room Wyatt slept in while living in Uganda is etched in my mind forever. It was tiny; there were three beds to probably eight or nine children. Wyatt shared a bed with maybe five other babies. They slept all lined up across the mattress. It makes me smile to think about; all these babies were living life together in the most physical way possible.

Grief has a way about it, it has to escape. Grief has to be lived through and my boy grieved at night. I don't know why, maybe one day we will, but there was something about the night. For months I sat beside him for hours as he screamed too afraid to fall asleep. I could tell you about the hours I sang to him, rubbed his back and eventually sat there crying alongside him as he wailed through his heartache. There were night terrors and kinds of screams you hear in the middle of the night that make your stomach hurt because sorrow has a sound about it. For almost a solid year Dustin sat in his room for hours waiting for him to fall asleep and always ended up back in there in the middle of the night sleeping beside that scared, grieving boy. Wyatt used to call his bed "daddy's bed" because that's how many nights Dustin slept beside Wyatt. The day he courageously decided to sleep in his big boy bed all by himself I could have burst with pride. The night the grief was silenced leaves my heart a little weepy.

There are not many spaces in this life where I can so clearly see the hand of God than within the space of adoption. Jesus does redeem, restore and heal little hearts. He does, I've seen it. Jesus really can grow a heart to love. He can, I've lived it. It's holy ground, this bearing witness to redemption. It's sacred, experiencing restoration. He trades beauty for ashes every time, and to think we could have missed this.

10

EGG ROLLS & SACRED SPACES

It was hard at first to not think about JT when I looked at Wyatt, but every time I looked at Wyatt I saw JT and my heart wasn't sure what to do with it. Their stories overlapped, and at the same time, their stories were very separate. Both of their stories take up space in my heart, its different space but it is space nonetheless. The memory of JT will never be more significant than Wyatt, but there would also be no Wyatt if there hadn't first been a JT. There was so much tension right there, and I couldn't decide if it was wrong or sacred.

My last night in Uganda was a hard one. Wyatt had finally fallen asleep. I had Taylor Swift on as loud as I could play it without waking him up. I had just finished packing up all of our things and was drinking my last Nile Special. I sat at my kitchen table trying to write an email that would tell a lot of people where I had been for the last two and a half months and what I had been doing. I was trying to form words around introducing our child for the first time and all of a sudden I couldn't stop crying. Like, head in my hands, possibly making an audible noise, for real couldn't stop kind of crying. I felt so relieved and so overwhelmed and so excited and so sad. I sent Dustin an email that said, "I'm so excited about Wyatt and I feel so sad about JT. It's the first time I've let myself feel both of those at the same time since I've been here. I can't stop crying." His response was so perfect. He said, "Yeah, it's hard because that part of the story will always suck." And that's the truth. The Wyatt part of the story will always, always be exciting and the JT part of the story will always, always suck. It's both. It will always be both. Those two boys are intertwined in a way they will never fully understand.

This journey was teaching me a lot about granting permission; how so often we don't allow ourselves and others the space to feel life the way it happens. How uncomfortable it can be to admit we are not excited about something exciting. How awkward it can be to sit across from someone who admits that. We are so into happy endings; we're constantly searching for redemption, silver linings and for things to make sense that we can so easily miss out on the beauty and the tension of life itself.

Adopting Wyatt was teaching me that having a child in our home would never fix what happened with JT. Wyatt did not provide us with closure, and he did not give us peace about what happened. Adopting him didn't help us make any more sense of it all or understand why it happened; Wyatt didn't heal the pain we felt about JT. Wyatt did not save our adoption story or make it whole, and he most certainly didn't redeem it. I was learning those are things that Jesus does and the minute I think a child can do those things for me I've missed it entirely.

I sat in my therapist's office one afternoon and told her how I had recently lost my mind one night at dinner over egg rolls. I told her it wasn't even about the egg rolls, because the thing we lose our mind over is never really the thing, right? Instead, it was about the last few years, about motherhood and adoption and how exactly none of it was what I thought it would be. People talk about adoption as if it makes sense and is full of rainbows, but that wasn't what I was living. Nothing made sense inside the walls of my home. It was all so ugly and so hard. It felt like we were living in wreckage or navigating shark-infested waters or quite possibly both at the same time. The hard part, it turns out, had not been completing an adoption but rather turning strangers into a family. We had put our heads down, just solely surviving, barely breathing for so many months after coming home, and then one day we stopped surviving and started functioning as a typical family. I didn't know what to do with any of that.

I told her adoption had not been what I wanted it to be. I knew in my head how challenging it could be but how hellishly hard it had all really been to live. How traumatic those months in Uganda by myself had felt and how unjustifiably angry at Dustin I was because he hadn't (couldn't) been there. How impossible it had been to bond with a baby who didn't really like you at first. How much shame and anger I felt. How hard it was not to take a baby's grief so deeply, deeply personal. How cruel and isolating it at times all felt. How paralyzed in fear I was at parenting him. How much I silently struggled with not being the mom I thought I would be. How I thought being a mom would make me so much happier than it had. How crippling it was to want to own all of this and move forward, and how damaging it was not to be able to.

Becoming a mother had done a number on me; I lost a part of myself, and I wasn't sure how to cope. I was so afraid of messing everything up; afraid of messing him up. I was overwhelmed with constant feelings of shame, fear, and guilt. I had thought being a mom would be tremendously fun and satisfying. I thought I would feel fulfilled and at peace with this new role in life. If I'm honest, I thought it would be easy. I figured it would be easy to transition from working full time to all of a sudden staying at home full time with a small child I was still getting to know. I believed deep down I would love being a mom straight out of the gate. Except it hadn't been any of those things and instead been more like the exact opposite. Instead, motherhood had felt awkward- it didn't feel natural. I felt like a fake and more like a babysitter than a mom.

I sat there on her couch that day admitting things I had only kept hidden deep inside me. I acknowledged how ridiculous and embarrassing some of this felt and also how cruel I believed it to be to ignore any longer. The longer I talked the freer I felt. Therapy is gold. At one point she looked at me and said, "Have you grieved all of this yet? Have you given yourself permission to grieve that adoption and motherhood have not been what you expected or wanted them to be?"

Who grieves the beautiful life you have just because it's not exactly what you thought it would be? The idea felt awkward and audacious and a little bit rebellious. It quite frankly didn't make much sense, but sometimes you must grieve beautiful things in order to see them as something beautiful. Sometimes you must mourn the person you thought you'd be in order to step into the person you are. Sometimes you must grieve the people who are not in your family so you can adore those who are in it. Sometimes we must permit ourselves to mourn the life you hoped for, wash your face off and hold tight to the life you have.

I burst into tears one night at dinner over JT. I hadn't cried about him since that night in Uganda, but for some reason it hit me, and I burst into tears because it was all still so weird. It's an odd thing, losing a child and then gaining one. I think about him always, and I think about him never. Life looks so different, and it feels so right and yet there is still this tiny little JT size hole that will always make me wonder what life would have been like with him. I wonder what he looks like now and what his favorite color is. I wonder what his favorite subject is and if he still has that contagious laugh. I wonder where he is right now and if he still gives great hugs. When you lose something that is still living it can make you wonder sometimes, and so sometimes I do.

We don't talk about him very much anymore and I don't always think about him. I don't pray for him every single day like I once was convinced I would. My heart doesn't physically hurt anymore.

I feel a little bit sad about all of that, and I also feel okay about all of that, too. I bought a wind chime and hung it up in our backyard in his honor. My heart needed to acknowledge him, and for no particular reason, a wind chime made sense. Wyatt and I went to the store and chose the perfect one; I hung it up when we got home. That night after dinner I took my phone out and snapped a picture of the wind chime hanging up with Wyatt jumping on the trampoline in the background and that red tricycle sitting in the driveway. As I stood in my backyard watching the sun go down, I felt peace. This life is stunningly beautiful, and it is also ruthlessly brutal. I'm okay with that.

11

I WANT YOU TO KNOW

Hey Sister,

It's Mother's Day, and I'm thinking about you. I wish you were here. I wish the two of you could be together. I wish he could bring you some handpicked flowers and give you a sweaty kiss. I wish he could wish you a happy Mother's Day and tell you he loves you in his tiny voice. I wish he could see himself in your eyes and your smile and hear himself in your voice and your laughter. I want you to know him.

I want you to know that you birthed one heck of a little boy. He's almost two now, and he deserves a trophy for being a toddler. He is determined to do every last thing by himself, and it is surprisingly my fault when he can't. He likes to tell me to cut his banana up and then refuse to eat it because he didn't want it cut up. He is stubborn as all get out. He can throw a really good tantrum. The age of two is fun. And by "fun" I mean confusing.

I want you to know the feet that kicked around in your belly are the squishiest feet I've seen. Those feet learned to walk by pushing a trash can around. He thought it was the funniest thing ever. That boy of yours never stops moving. Those feet were made to run. They were also made to dance. I don't know if he got his dance moves from you or not, but the child can move. That boy of yours has dimples and a great, big smile. He has deep brown eyes that almost sparkle. We've worked hard for that sparkle. He's happy.

I want you to know your boy is kind. He doesn't like to share much and can be sort of mean sometimes, but I hear that's pretty normal. I think he will make a great friend one day. He is crazy smart. He is hilarious, and he knows it. His laugh is delicious. His fake laugh is killer. He has the most beautiful eyelashes that curl all the way up to his eyelids. I feel jealous of those eyelashes. He has this look where he cuts his eyes and smirks and every time I feel like we may be in trouble one day.

I want you to know your boy loves cars. He has at least two in his hands at all times. He learned to ride a tricycle and thinks he's hot stuff. He likes to jump on the trampoline and play with a big red ball. He loves to throw rocks into a lake by our house. You can always make him laugh by blowing bubbles. He loves to read. He's sleeping in a big boy bed now, it has trucks all over it, and I'm proud of him. He wakes up asking for popsicles. He loves slushies, he usually picks purple, but sometimes it's red or blue. Bacon is the name of his game right now.

I want you to know he is loved. He is being taken care of. I wasn't sure he would ever be truly happy, but I think he is. He's brave, that boy of yours. I want you to know that you are loved, too. You will always be the first. He will always be yours. I'm not afraid of you; you will always be spoken of in this house. We talk about you often. It's confusing, and I know it will continue to be, but I think it's important. You will never be a secret, and you will never be forgotten. I respect you, and my heart aches for you; the decision you had to make. I hope you get to hold this sweet boy of yours one day.

I want you to know we believe in a whole lot of grace. Your boy has made me believe in redemption, so we believe in that, too. It is a privilege, an honor, to be one of his moms. I want you to know this little boy of ours is just that, ours, and I will be eternally grateful for you. Thank you for sharing him with me.

Happy Mother's Day.

12

CRYING BABIES & PAPER BAGS

Dustin called one day and asked what we were doing. We were driving home from the playground technically, but I responded with, "Well, Dustin. I'm currently driving home to put a paper bag over my head." He then, cautiously, asked why Wyatt was crying in the background and how the day had been. I was very calm and kind and non-emotional as I responded over the screams of my child in the back seat with, "How has the day been? That is an adorable question. Thank you very much for asking. Wyatt has literally cried all day. He woke up crying, and I feel confident we are going to put him to bed crying. He has thrown exactly thirty-seven raging tantrums and has had twenty-nine meltdowns. The latest being in the middle of the street while I changed his blow out diaper in some random person's front yard because poop really was everywhere.

So he's screaming because I changed his diaper? Wouldn't let him eat a book this morning? I tried to feed him something other than Teddy Graham's today at lunch? He rolled his car under the couch after I had told him a bazillion times I wasn't going to get it anymore? Wouldn't let him eat the toilet paper roll he got out of the trash? Told him he couldn't throw balls at the TV? Oh, no those were all earlier. He is currently screaming because he can't have my keys because I'm driving. I have crap all over me and a headache. I cannot "redirect" anymore today. I cannot deal with the redirection; that mess is for the birds. I'm about to lose my mind. So I'm going home to put a paper bag over my head and wait for you to get home."

Being a mom can really bring out the best in a girl. I heard people say things like, "It's so funny when toddlers get frustrated!" Or "I just laugh when my child refuses to comply with anything good and holy!" Or "When my toddler throws a tantrum in the grocery store I just think it's so cute." Or "Aw, sweet Wyatt's a crier? Aw." I did not think these things, and I thought those people might be on drugs. All the irrational crying did was make me sweaty. I didn't really feel like laughing, and I most certainly didn't think it was cute or "aww." My heart would start beating fast, and I would get extremely hot; I felt the sudden urge to scratch my ears off. Maybe I have a sensory thing. The never-ending crying made me all kinds of panicky and anxious.

But I was driving home to put a paper bag over my head

because I read a story once about a fellow mom who did not do so well with the crying and the tantrums and the, "We were having such a fun time! What just happened?" moments of motherhood. She didn't love them, and shockingly she didn't even like them. Those moments made her feel like a crazy person, and so her solution was to put a paper bag over her head. Why? I don't know. You really should not need an explanation all the time in motherhood. Her children were still in the same room screaming, but she just had a paper bag over her head. She even drew a smiley face on the front of the bag so her children would remember these times as happy. Most of the times her children were so caught off guard by this move they stopped crying altogether. Sometimes they did not. The paper bag itself did not change one thing about the utter chaos ensuing around her, but for some reason it made her feel less psycho and more stable inside of her paper bag.

I remember reading this story before I had children thinking, *Good Lord. I will surely never feel like that or need to do that. My kids will be well behaved and never cry because I am going to nail motherhood. That's so funny though that she feels like that and needs to do that. I will laugh at this because this will never be me.* But then this day happened, and I remembered the paper bag story. I found myself not nailing motherhood, and I felt crazy and frazzled. I had human feces on me. My child had no chill. I felt like he enjoyed making me question my will to live and so I went home and put a paper bag over my head. I didn't care. This was the line being drawn in the sand. If Wyatt would not stop screaming over the fact that the sun was orange and not purple like he wanted it to be then this was going to be our new normal. Carry on.

And you know what? It was amazing. Nothing changed about my current situation, Wyatt was still crying because someone had painted our front door red before we moved here and he wanted it to be blue, but I didn't care! It felt less like the world is ending and more like it is all okay inside of this paper bag. It also made me giggle and would eventually make the crying stop because what is actually going on here?

Motherhood is insane. It's something you can't prepare for no matter how many books you read. I wish I had known this earlier. You will live through the toddler years. You may not like them, and there's nothing wrong with that. It will feel like you are holding your breath underwater but you will survive them, and then you will come up for air when they are four, and it will be better. There will be things you find yourself missing about toddlerhood, though. Like, their little voice or the way they said words wrong or their love for something as simple as picking flowers. And then there will be things you do not miss like asking your child forty times if they are sure they want a green popsicle and watching them confirm their choice and eat it, only to throw their tiny body down on the ground weeping because they wanted to pick purple.

13

BECAUSE LAUGHING IS BETTER THAN CRYING

Dear Wyatt,

Right now you are four and a half years old, and I like you so much. I heard four was a promising age and I have to say you've hit a sweet spot. You are charming and witty. You're so smart. You are mostly kind. You sleep through the night and for that alone I want to smother you with hugs. You call me your best girl. You can communicate with intellectual words that make sense as they come out of your mouth and go into my ears. You are a joy right now.

I don't want you to think you have always been a gem, though. That might make you cocky or give you a big head or something like that. While you are a Precious Lamb currently, you used to be a toddler and more like an Angry Beaver. You were incredibly self-centered, always requesting "up please" and for us to stay awake with you every minute of the nighttime hours. You were demanding and quite honestly a little crazed. There was one time you asked me to cut up your hotdog, and like an idiot, I did as instructed only to find out that by "cut up" you meant "not cut up." The way you looked at me sent a chill down my spine I clearly have not forgotten. Someone wrote a book entitled, "Toddlers Are A-holes" and while I don't really feel like we should call people a-holes to their faces, I have to agree.

I wanted to take some time to tell you a little bit about yourself as a ruthless toddler. Don't get fussy; I am still processing your toddler-hood. Like the time I debated peeing on myself because I didn't want to wake you up from a coveted car nap. I can't help you understand.

One day I created a game where I laid down, and you rolled cars across my back while my eyes were closed. Sometimes I would ask you to roll them harder in certain spots because you were basically giving me a much needed massage while I took a nap. I need you to know this felt like the definition of winning.

There were days I would find you scouring the trashcan like a raccoon trying to eat the toilet paper roll. I found you licking the toilet on more occasions than I care to remember. You were hell bent on playing with knives. You would frequently request pasta for breakfast. Most of these things all happened while I blinked and usually occurred before 7:30 a.m., so that felt mostly like time well spent.

One time you elbowed me so hard in the chest you burst a blood vessel. It felt kind of aggressive and rude looking back. That is the same time I sent your dad real, authentic tears via text message. The time I wouldn't let you play with your baby doll because you pooped on him was a fun day except it wasn't. I almost gave in and let you play with a doll that had human feces on it because you were so angry at me. You were not here for logic or things like sanitation; you wanted what you wanted, and you made sure everyone in your path questioned their will to live if you did not get it.

I learned that "mommy play!" was the cutest invitation to come sit and do everything wrong. I would eat the pretend food you served me incorrectly. I rolled cars the wrong way and built LEGOS not to your high standard. You brought me books to read and then informed me I was reading them wrong. One time I even wiped your tears off wrong. I didn't even know these were things. You kept me humble.

I have to tell you my favorite thing about you being a toddler was that you changed your mind every .01 seconds and never shared this new information with me. And by "favorite" I mean I only almost overdosed on Advil twice. One week you survived by eating only blueberries. It was fine. The next week Kroger had a two for five dollar deal on blueberries, and I thought, "Perfect! Wyatt loves blueberries!" That was the week you no longer liked blueberries. Every day was Opposite Day, and we just sat around waiting for the hand to strike. *He asked for a banana. Does that mean he really wants an orange? Or maybe a sandwich? Oh, God. What if I hand him a banana? What if I don't hand him a banana?* You cried when it was time to take a bath and then you sobbed when it was time to get out.

I loved picking you up from your grandparent's house because they got all braggy about you. *He was perfect! He slept nineteen hours straight last night! He ate arugula and asked for more! He didn't throw any tantrums! He wrote the first draft of his college essay!* While I was over here not sure if I was breathing wrong to you, over there they thought you were the eighth wonder of the world. It felt special.

Trying to explain anything to you only felt like a poor use of time. I feel sure this is what the Bible is talking about when referring to "weeping and gnashing of teeth." The summer I tried to explain "rest period" to you was basically like I was talking to an annoyed napkin. A canceled play date? I would have rather cut through my arm tendon like the guy stuck in a cave in *127 Hours*. The time I stood staring at you trying to explain that I didn't understand what, "I want to drink my slushy inside-outside" meant made want to volunteer as tribute in The Hunger Games.

You were so gifted at being a toddler. You excelled. You simultaneously made me want to sob uncontrollably while lying in the fetal position and eat your face off because you were so squishy and cute. You deserve a trophy, dude. I love you so much, Baby Wyatt. I also like that you are not a toddler anymore and trying to scratch the moles off my face. Rest in peace toddler years; don't let the door hit you on the way out.

Love,

Your Best Girl

14

HOW TO BE A PARENT

I sat in my therapist's office one week sobbing over being a parent. I didn't know how to be a parent, and the world was telling me one hundred ways to do it that all contradicted themselves. All of my friends were parenting differently, and I didn't know where I stood. The adoption books told me to do everything this way, but my personality was not wired for that all the time, and so instead of trying something to see if it worked or not I did nothing. Instead of figuring out how to parent best with the personalities on the table I stood there frozen.

My counselor finally looked at me and said, "Where is the Courtney I met all those years ago? The one who did not care about what other people did or said? Where did she go?" The truth was she was right. I had lost her. She had gotten dragged to the ground and was lying under all of the stupid crap out there that tells us how to be a parent. I was almost mad about it. But it made sense, too. We are a group of parents who are inundated with information. At times we can have too much data. We are always doing something wrong because there is an article that tells us so and a study to back it up.

I stood in my parent's lake house one morning cooking eggs with my mom. Dustin and I had been up all night with Wyatt. Neither one of us could get him to go to sleep, so we stood downstairs in the house full of sleeping people whisper arguing over it all. *Why won't he go to sleep! It's 2:00 in the morning, I don't know! Make him stop crying! I can't! What are we supposed to do? Its 4 AM I don't know! I hate this! So do I!* I asked my mom if her and my dad had ever argued over raising my two sisters and me. She snorted laughter into the skillet. Of course, they had. But they also had just done the best they could and prayed some of it would stick.

I spent the next few months unsubscribing to every parenting resource that was flooding my inbox. I unfollowed every mom page on Instagram and even left every single adoption related parenting group on Facebook. I stopped buying parenting books and refused to read one article that spoke on the subject of how to raise children. Because while there are some excellent resources out there helping each of us navigate this whole parenting gig, I had gotten lost somewhere in the endless information telling me how to do a job that only I truly knew how to do best.

I began to remember who I was; the person who had been

killed in the process of becoming a mom. I was reminded that our personalities were God-given and not an accident. They are not to be squashed simply because we have become parents. They can be fine-tuned, for sure; we are all works in progress but smashed? No way. It is okay to be funny and a mom. It's okay to be sarcastic. It's okay not to be precious and it's okay not to raise precious kids. We need some spice or the world would be mind-boggling boring. It's okay to change your mind as a parent, and it is okay not to know exactly what to do. It's okay to take a toy away, and it's okay to let your child cry. It's okay to feed your child organic foods, and it's also okay if they like Cheetos. It's okay to say you are sorry to a two-year-old. It's okay to raise your voice sometimes; no one is going to die because of it. It's okay to turn into Ursula from *The Little Mermaid* when you're child wakes up for the day at 4:26 AM every day because that is freaking early. It's okay for your child to be mad at you sometimes. I spent years mad at my parents because they wouldn't let me read *Harry Potter* or watch MTV. I was beginning to learn we're all just making it up as we go. We could all do ourselves a favor and chill out a little bit. Two-year-olds hit and suck at sharing, and sometimes you might lose your patience over it all. Get over it, apologize when you need to and move on.

This is for all of us who got lost in the parenting books and studies and classes and what everyone else is saying and doing. This is for all of us who found ourselves again. Because being a parent is hard enough without all the extra noise out there telling you how to be a parent to the kid only you know best. So here is a comprehensive list of all the information on how to be a parent to a toddler in 19 steps. Hope this is helpful.

1. Do not give your baby formula under any circumstances. I cannot list all the reasons why here because it would take up the rest of the pages in this book. Breast is always, always best. Unless that is not an option for you and then the formula is great. It is so good to give your child the nutrients they need in whatever form available to you. But breast is preferred, and you will be judged should you adopt a child who needs a bottle and you are seen putting the packaged powder into his mouth because producing milk from your body was not a part of the adoption requirements.

2. Do not ever put your child down. You should wear them at all times in a baby carrier preferably on your chest with your child staring into your eyes. This is nurturing the bond between you two and increases their felt safety. If your body begins to experience severe pains because of this, you are doing it right. You should put your child down because this helps them learn to crawl and walk and do things on their own which will increase independence and it will be the downfall of your attachment with them. You should most likely wear your baby until they go to middle school.

3. You should come up with a routine and stick with it always. Children thrive on routine and spontaneity. Schedules are essential for children that should be kept exactly always and never.

4. Do not leave your child in a room by themselves to fall asleep. Unless you want them to learn to self-soothe which is a great coping skill that also makes children feel abandoned and like they are going to be eaten by Voldemort.

5. Do not put your child in time out. It is scientifically proven

to be ineffective and damaging to your child's heart. You will destroy your child as a human being if you place them in time out. Instead, place them in a "time in" where you sit with them. Do this as an alternative even if you are making dinner and your food is burning on the stove because you are sitting in time in with your child because of a sad choice they made. Children do not ever make sad choices only happy choices that just weren't happy at the time. It is okay to use time out as a discipline strategy if it works for you but know it hurts their hearts.

6.   Always speak to your children as Mother Theresa would. Do not raise your voice ever. Raising your voice causes your child to undergo unnecessary trauma. They will end up in counseling over this. If you are ever to get mad at your beloved child, you should always speak as if you are singing a song. This is good for their brains. It is also okay to raise your voice because you are human and sometimes people yell. But please understand that these incidents should be kept to a minimum.

7.   You should be aware of your parenting triggers before you become a parent. Is it crying? Whining? Being completely sleep deprived? Maybe all of the above? Again, you should know these before having children. Do not give in to your triggers. Keep your cool always. Do not get frustrated. Losing your cool will guarantee a lifetime of counseling for your child as stated above. It will also give them the same triggers you have when they have their own children. You should also relax because children can tell when their parents are stressed.

8.   Always give your child 13 bazillion choices. Any more than

13 bazillion and you are encouraging entitlement. Any less than 13 bazillion and you're just being plain neglectful.

9.   Do not avert your eyes from your child at any time during the day. They are the center of your world; you only have what feels like five years underwater with them before they leave you for kindergarten. Enjoy every last second. If you do have the audacity to let your eyes wander from your jewel, well done, you are a monster.

10.   When your child is throwing a tantrum, do not show any signs of anything on your face. Always remain neutral. If you laugh, that gives them a positive reaction, and they will continue to throw down. If you show frustration that gives them a negative reaction which makes their brain go into flight or fight mode. Leave them alone. Stay with them. Let them throw a tantrum and ignore them. Put them in a safe place and let them work it out. Contain them with your arms, rocking back and forth and whispering words of love in their ears.

11.   Your child should watch TV anywhere from no minutes a day up to three hours. It's best for their brains if they see no electronic screen until five years of age. One hour of TV a day starting at age two is good for your child. Thirty minutes of TV is best starting at age one.

12.   When playing with your child always let them lead. Your child is in charge and should make all play related decisions. Do not ever decline an invitation to play. You should always feel excited to eat pretend food and watch really boring puppet shows for absurd amounts of time. It is fine to let your child play alone as

this fosters independent play which is a developmental milestone. It is okay not to be always excited to play with your child because sometimes you don't want to and also it can be boring.

13.   Do not do things for your child if they can do it themselves. They will never be able to grow into functioning adults. Continue to do everything for your child. They need you, and this is nurturing for your child's relationship with you. If you want your child to be able to launch from your home and be a productive member of society in the future you should continue doing everything always and never for your child.

14.   Do not ever say no to your child. You should always say yes. Unless you can't say yes for safety reasons, then you should come up with a creative way to not say no. You should tell your child no sometimes as this helps them understand rules and boundaries and also helps them understand they are not in charge of everything. Do not negotiate with your child but instead communicate to them who is the boss. Say yes exactly 20 times a day as this fills their love tank.

15.   Use sticker charts as a way to reward your child for their behavior. Do not use sticker charts as a way to reward your child. Don't reward your child for anything. This causes entitlement, and you can expect your child to live with you forever. Reward your child always with a party.

16.   Sometimes you will need to go with your gut. You will need to make in the moment decisions with and for your child. You should always prepare for these situations even if you do not know what they will ever be. Every single moment is a teachable

one that will make or break your child. Do not mess up. Feel confident in yourself!

17.   Don't ever wake your child up. Unless they are napping and you want them to sleep at night. A child should nap between 1.5-3 hours daily. There should be exactly 5 hours in between the morning wake up, nap, and bedtime. Do not make your child go to sleep. They will tell you when and if they are tired even if they never tell you that because they don't want to go to sleep. Your child needs 8-10 hours of sleep every single night as this is best for their health and development.

18.   You should cherish every moment of parenting. Parenting your children is a grace that you should also not feel pressured to enjoy every moment because that's ludicrous. Enjoy every single moment always and sometimes.

19. When in doubt, Google it. Except don't because that is where this list came from.

Carry on. You've totally got this.

15

GO FORTH & HAVE NO FEAR

The second I walked off the plane with Wyatt I knew we would adopt again; I didn't know from where or when but I knew without a doubt we were not done. As we were living life in the weeds, life after the airport, I knew there would be more children added to this mix. While we were doing the work of becoming a family I believed deep in my soul, we would one day do the work of becoming a family all over again.

About six months after Wyatt had been stateside I looked at Dustin and said, "I need you to know I don't necessarily want to do this right now, but I think we're supposed to adopt again." He did not agree this time. He pushed back. "No way," he said. He thought it would be crazy to do again. We were finally getting settled into being a family of three; why rock the boat? We did not see eye to eye this time, not at all. For months we argued. I cried more than once. I could not explain the feeling I had that we were supposed to do this again. We sat on our front porch one night hashing out the reality of adopting again. He thought it would be too hard to do again. He questioned why I would even want to do it again after everything had been so challenging before. I had to remind him that I really didn't want to do it again but I believed we were supposed to. We said all the wrong things to each other. We got so mad that night. I'm confident our neighbors heard us speaking in loud voices to one another. We eventually dropped it and moved on. Neither one of us dared bring it up again. But I could not shake that nagging feeling.

It's time again.

We sat on the couch watching TV one night when out of nowhere Dustin said, "Why don't you email the adoption agency we used with Wyatt and just see if they have any kids who are waiting for a family." I looked him square in the eyes and said, "You know they are going to have waiting kids. There are almost always waiting kids. Do you really want me to do that?" Sure enough, there were waiting kids. Conversation re-opened.

I always knew our family would grow through adoption-multiple ones. We knew we wanted Wyatt to share the same skin color as other people in our family. I so desperately wanted Wyatt to share something with a sibling, and I desperately wanted that something to be Uganda. We knew this was what we were supposed to do. We almost talked ourselves out it, though. I can't tell you how many times we looked at each other and said, "Are we crazy? Are you still okay with this? Are we about to screw everything up?"

I didn't want to go back to Uganda. I wanted Wyatt to share Uganda with a sibling, but we had been through a lot there. It all still felt a little too raw for me. I thought we could adopt another black child or a child from Africa; they would be able to share in those things, but I didn't know if I had it in me to go back to Uganda. I thought surely there was another way. I spent countless hours looking at other countries. I had phone calls with friends who were doing foster care. I talked with our local department of child services. We were on the fence for a real minute about adopting a sibling set of four from Ethiopia. For months we researched, and I felt no peace about any of it. This is not what we're supposed to do. And then that night on the couch we circled back to Uganda, and it felt right. Peace. Sometimes the thing you're supposed to do is not exactly what you want to do. Sometimes you have to do things that scare you all over again.

The hard thing about adoption for me is that it's so easy to say no. It's beyond easy to agonize and overthink it. There are a million different ways you can talk yourself out of it. Your house isn't big enough, what about the other kids, we aren't equipped, it feels scary, on and on you can go. There are four trillion legitimate reasons to be scared and apprehensive and want to call it quits on the whole dang thing. But when I looked at our life- our house, our families, our people-there was so much laughter and love and goodness to go around. I couldn't stop thinking about how much it wasn't all that crazy to want to share it with another little human being who needed a family.

Wyatt's social worker came over one afternoon to do a home visit. Wyatt heard her car as she pulled in the driveway and ran to open the door for her. She hugged me as she came inside, sat down on my couch and let Wyatt roll cars across her arms. We talked about how we were doing- how Wyatt was doing. She helped us through some struggles and was thrilled for certain developments. At one point I looked at her and said, "You're going to think we're crazy but we're going to adopt again." She laughed, said she had heard crazier and began the paperwork for us to do it again. It felt exactly right.

Not long after that, I texted a friend to tell her what was going on and she said, "I'm excited to see God weave another beautifully broken and redemptive story into your lives again." I had never felt less qualified to do exactly that, but I had also learned you didn't need to be super qualified to open your home up to someone who needed one. You didn't need to be a superhero to be able to love one more. We said yes one more time and began again.

We had always been open to adopting siblings. A group of siblings can be harder to find a family for because there's more than one and so we always said we were open to that possibility. But more than one child was never given to us, so we always said yes to the one. I will never forget being at the park down the street from our house one afternoon with Wyatt when I got a message from our adoption agency that read, "I know you guys are open to two. How open to two are you really?" I immediately texted Dustin something to the tune of, "Holy crap are we open to two kids? Like REALLY open to it? If we are they've got twins waiting." He responded with a solid and confident, "Yes." While I freaked out, *we're open to two. Yes. Right? We're open to two. Wait. TWO? Two whole people. That is scary. But it's not. We've always been open to two. We can't say no just because it's two of them. I mean we CAN say no but why would we other than because it's scary and sounds hard. But, hi, one is scary and is hard. WE'RE OPEN TO TWO. Yes.*

Yes.

A few months later, Dustin and I landed in Uganda late into the night ready to meet the twins the following day. We exited the plane into that all familiar Ugandan air. It was cold that night; it must have rained that day, I had to reach into my backpack and pull out my jacket. We walked across the tarmac, entered the airport and stood in line to get our visas. The guard pointed for us to go to the next window, we walked up and slid our passports across the counter. The woman behind the computer typed away, asked how Wyatt was and asked for our fingerprints. She stamped our passports; we grabbed our luggage and met our friend Steven outside the airport. We drove windows down, through the streets of Uganda. I watched out my window at the all familiar scene of night in Uganda, music blaring on every corner and people everywhere. There were women in salons doing hair and people sitting on the ground selling shoes and soccer jerseys. The bodas swerved in and out of traffic, and pedestrians wandered through the middle of the road. The breeze, the sounds and the smell of street life made my heart happy to be back on the red dirt again. I felt at peace. We crawled into our bed that night listening to the sounds of Uganda underneath our mosquito net and I knew what we were doing was what we were supposed to be doing.

A few hours later we were back in the car and on the road, and as we pulled up to the orphanage, I looked out the window and saw a herd of small children gathered in the front yard sitting in a crowd of sorts. I wondered if they were over there. We got out of the car and were greeted by several nuns who ran the orphanage where our children had been living. She walked us over to the group of kids and asked us to pick out who we thought our children were. I said, "Are you serious?" It was a joke; she thought it would be funny, I was horrified. We had seen one picture of the twins, and there was no telling how old they were in that picture. I have never felt more pressure in all of my life. We scanned the crowd of bald heads and brown faces- we got one child right and one child wrong.

For days they didn't say a word. I wondered if they could talk. They never cried, I thought we had hit the jackpot. All they wanted to do was be held, and so for days, we held those two silent two-year-olds not having a clue what was to come. I don't think I will ever forget the peace I felt pulling out of that orphanage with the two of them in our car the following day. It was not a feeling of peace that everything was going to be easy or make sense, but it was a sense of peace that these two belonged with us. I needed that confirmation then more than I ever knew I did. I would come back to it often in the months to follow.

Wyatt taught me that love is a choice and I can choose to do love before I feel love. It was one of the holiest, hardest lessons I could have ever learned from an eighteenth-month-old. The twins were about to teach me that sometimes the act of love comes at a cost. Sometimes love requires something from us. They were about to show me that there are times we may be asked to love as an act of service. The twins were going to teach me that sometimes God just might set your entire life on fire and ask you to stand there in flames for a good long while and proclaim, "He is good."

16

NOT YET

We flew home, and a few weeks later I went back for our court hearing. The day I stood in a scorching hot Ugandan courtroom for hours trying to prove to a judge that my husband and I were worthy to be granted legal guardianship of the twins was, how do I say this, comical. For three solid hours, I stood before a judge and was interrogated with questions. Some were legit questions like, "How will you teach them about Uganda?" and "Is your community diverse or will they be the only black kids?" and "Tell me why I should send these black immigrant children to a place that has voted for a man who vocally hates black people and immigrants?" Some questions were laugh out loud absurd like; "Tell me how I am supposed to believe you can financially care for these children when you have student loan debt?" and "Can you even afford to feed them if you can't afford to buy a Porsche?" Other questions were so widely inappropriate I cannot even write them down. Let's just say I had a charming conversation surrounding the topic of intercourse because, "If you do not have biological children you must be having sex wrong. Let me tell you a few things," and now a room full of Ugandans know every last intimate detail about my sex life. Fun! This man was relentless. He pressed on for one hundred and eighty minutes which felt like an exact lifetime. I cursed and I sweated through my entire dress. One child tried to climb out the second story window. I looked down at one point and found them both asleep, face down on the tile floor.

We had spent the entire day previously waiting to be seen by the judge. For seven hours I paced around a building attempting to entertain two children who didn't understand anything I was saying and wanted nothing to do with me. I was by myself with twins whose activity of choice was screaming while running away from me in opposite directions. For seven whole hours, I chased after them with a crazed look in my eye. We were a sight to bear witness to; a sweaty, crazy white lady yelling English words while running after two screaming Ugandan toddlers who were shouting things back in their native language. Then the judge declared he was too tired to see us and to come back the following day. Life felt rude that day. But come back the next day we did where we repeated the acts of the day before for five hours while we waited for the judge to arrive at his chambers. We were finally seen and granted legal guardianship of the twins, and I only feel slightly traumatized from the whole ordeal. Therapy is helping. Sometimes the only thing left to do is laugh while you cry.

I would end up going home and coming back again for a third time. I thought this trip would be my last; that I would board a plane home in a few weeks with every single one of my children beside me. I decided to bring Wyatt with me. I thought it would be fun. I thought he would be helpful. I thought it would make some of it more manageable. For the record, it did none of those things. Someone asked me once why I did that and I replied, "Well, I thought they would be friends?"

The day the twins foster parents dropped them off at our house was one of the worst days of my life. They had to be pried off of our precious friends who had been caring for them for months. They screamed terrified, guttural screams I had never heard before. They banged their heads against the door as they watched the only mom and dad they had ever known walk away. I tried everything-singing, distracting, holding, a movie, food- nothing worked. They eventually escaped from our house and went sprinting away from me and after their foster parents. I chased after them, grabbed hold of their screaming, flailing bodies and settled in the parking lot of our compound as we watched them drive away. I rocked them back and forth; my heart was pounding, tears were streaming down my face as I whispered, "This is hard. This is hard. I know this is hard. We're going to be okay. This is hard. This is hard." I don't know who I was whispering more to, myself or them.

For the next three weeks, I lived some of the worst weeks of my life. Not one of us liked each other. I had three two-year-olds who hated each other's very existence. The twins hated my very existence. I wasn't particularly fond of them either. Not one of us was living our best life during this time.

I cried and yelled and cussed. One time I straight up stuck my tongue out at one of my children while standing with my back to them because that is the state of emotional turmoil I was in. I stood over laundry scrubbing my anger out with my bare hands. I wept in the dark as I sat and rubbed backs and prayed the sovereign, holy Lord would close eyes and keep them shut until the morning. I sent Dustin 911 style text messages that read, "What have we done, this is BS, you need to get you're a$$ here now, and also I think I might be dead." I prayed urgent prayers like, "God get me through the next minute" and then I prayed that every minute for every last hour.

I broke up fights that were deadly. I cannot tell you what it is like to walk in on one of your children trying to strangle another one of your children just because they didn't like them. I cleaned up more blood than I particularly care to remember because of the scratching that occurred. My children would maul one another in a way that is not your typical sibling wrestling match. One child was so stressed out by all that was going on they started picking their eyelashes out. And then they moved on to their hair; I would wake up to patches of hair on the ground beside their bed and new bald spots every morning. The twins would point at me laughing and talking to each other in their native language. They wanted nothing to do with me. They didn't speak English or understand a word I said. I didn't speak their language or understand a word they said.

We couldn't communicate with each other. They refused to comply with anything good and holy.

I was spit on, bitten, had food chewed up and thrown at me, scratched, and run away from. We endured raging trauma tantrums for hours and hours a day. They were the most intense tantrums I had yet to experience. Anything and everything would send this child spiraling down the path of raging for hours at a time. The people who believe that kids will always eventually stop crying are wrong. Some kids do not stop until their body physically can take no more and it shuts itself down. There is something deeply painful about watching a child become violently overcome with grief knowing you can do nothing but ride the tsunami alongside them and fervently pray it doesn't wipe everyone in its path out. Sometimes pain runs so deep the only option is to scream your way through it. I put kids in one room with a movie while I sat outside another kid's room with my fingers in my ears, rocking back and forth, sobbing my eyes out. I guarded the trash can because kids who have always been hungry will eat out of it when you aren't looking. I walked into rooms and saw pillows being ripped apart with bare hands, toys being destroyed with teeth and paint being scratched off the wall and eaten. Wyatt begged to go home every hour. I begged Dustin to save me from this Lord of the Flies situation I found myself in. I thought we might die. We were a mess, but we survived. By the grace of God we lived. Hallelujah. Adoption can be costly in more ways than one.

But then we hit a delay I thought would end it all and I packed them up and put them in the car with my friend Steven; I kissed their foreheads, and we all waved goodbye. It took me a few days to recover, but as Wyatt and I flew back home without the newest members of our family, I was able to remember that while those three weeks had been ugly and messy, they had also been full of laughter. I watched kids dance in the African rain. I read bedtime stories and sang little people to sleep. I blew a lot of bubbles. I played tag and peek-a-boo and made animal noises for days. I tickled so many tickles. I watched God ordained siblings who did not speak the same language start learning the art of being a sibling. I heard the word "mommy" uttered after weeks of not being called anything.

As I was driving to the airport with my oldest sitting on my lap, I found myself yet again reminded that God was good. I wasn't singing his praises yet, but I did believe he was good even in the delays. He was good even in the waiting and on the darkest of days where doubt, fear, and regret crept in. He was faithful even in the not yets of this life. As I boarded a plane home with only one of my children, I was reminded that God takes our yeses and molds us and stretches us in ways we could never have wanted or imagined.

17

PARTY OF FIVE

The journey to the twins was a hard one. It was long. We hit roadblocks and delays at every point. We jumped through hoops. I would end up traveling to Uganda almost every month for six consecutive months. I thought the delays would never come to an end. I had been in stand-offs with government authorities and screamed over emails and got sassy with government officials. I boarded flights out of Uganda not sure when or if I'd ever return. I tried to wrap my brain around being a family of five while at the same time recognizing that it might never happen.

That last time I came home from Uganda I was ready to walk away. We had hit yet another delay and this time I didn't know if I wanted to see this to completion. I was done; I had no more fight left in me. I had traveled to Uganda three times in four months, and I was physically exhausted. I was emotionally tired. I felt weary. I had experienced things alone I thought might haunt me forever. We had no more money. Every penny that had been allotted to this adoption had been cut into checks. Every penny not allotted to this adoption had been spent on all of the unexpected plane tickets and living expenses in Uganda. We had nothing left. I had left my wedding ring at home every single trip in case we needed to sell it. It's just the truth. Adoption is costly.

We sat around for a good long while talking about how much longer do we hang on? How much longer do we fight for this? At what point is it no longer wise or responsible to keep doing something when you have nothing left? Dustin made it clear he wasn't done yet. He told me he had a little bit of fight left in him. He said he wouldn't hang on forever, but he thought we should hang on a little bit longer.

I begrudgingly said okay and then spent a lot of time angry ranting to God. *I don't understand why this is happening. Do you hate us? Why do you continue to ask us to do things and then let them suck? I don't feel like that's very kind of you. Can't we do one thing that is easy? Just one would be nice. I don't want to keep doing this. You see our bank account. We have NOTHING LEFT. We can't afford to move there. We can't afford any more months of the twins living in foster care. We can't afford to fly back over there. I'm tired. Have you ever flown to Africa before, God? Because it hurts your body. Like, actually hurts it. I want to go on vacation. Yosemite, actually. Not Uganda. Exactly not Uganda. I don't want to keep doing this.*

One day I happened to be mindlessly scrolling through

Facebook and somewhere in between pictures of kids, food and political articles a quote popped up on my newsfeed about how if we pray for God to move mountains then we need to be prepared to wake up next to a shovel. The quote itself wasn't all that profound. The words didn't have much to do exactly with my precise situation but at that moment it hit me. Something fierce found resolve deep within my soul. What if fighting for something means hanging on a little bit longer? What if fighting for something doesn't always have to be big and brave and active? It can and is those things often but what if, sometimes, fighting is also those quiet moments of resolve not to give up yet? That is where I landed. I'll hang on quietly for a little bit longer. I will not give up yet.

For weeks we heard nothing, it was radio silent. I was convinced we had finally hit the roadblock that would end it all. It was such a stupid roadblock at that, something that had not one thing to do with the orphan status of either of our children. It wasn't even about ethics for God's sake! I had walked away from unethical cases before, and this was not that. This was dumb, but it was what was happening, and so we waited. We stopped talking about it, about them. We settled into the routine of summer and kept moving through life because what else are you supposed to do really?

Then one random Sunday afternoon I felt it. Deep in my bones, I knew they were coming home. It was time. I can't explain it, but I knew. This roadblock was not the end. Our case was going to be approved. They were coming home. It was time to create space for them. I went on a cleaning rampage… closets, clothes, rooms, toys, books. I was on the warpath. Crossing me was unwise. If you didn't wear it or play with it or read it or touch it, it was going in a bag. I opened up the door to their room and painted the walls. I put sheets on the bed and hung the letters of their first names on the wall. In the middle of all of this Dustin asked me what I was doing and the only thing I could tell him was, "They're coming home. I feel it."

The next morning I woke up to an email saying they were moving forward with our case. Three days later I woke up to an email saying we were approved. We could bring them home with us. I'll hang on for just a little bit longer. Thank you, Jesus. These two matter. They were purposed, they were worth fighting for, and they were worth hanging on for.

I lay in bed those nights begging God to make a way. *So it's nice and all that we can go back to Uganda now, but we don't have enough money. Remember how many times I have had to fly over there? Do you remember that? Every single one of those flights costs dollar bills. What do you want us to do? Max out a credit card? Sell my wedding ring? How do we get back over there?* And every time I felt God whisper, "Ask." *Nope. Not interested. Give me another answer.* "Ask." *Can you not just rain down the dollars from heaven or let the airlines give us our plane tickets for free? I mean you made a blind man see! You can let us fly for free.* "Ask." *Come on. I don't want to. Please give me a different answer. I'll donate plasma or something.* "Ask." *I would rather not. We can eat sandwiches for seven years.* "Ask." *Oh my gosh, God. Do you even hear me? I do not want to ask! Can you not burden someone somewhere to send us the exact amount of money and let it land in our mailbox tomorrow? You've done it before.* "Ask."

When the Lord tells you to do something, it's wise to do it. I asked and not even twenty- four hours later people had rallied in one of the most significant moves of solidarity ever to get us back on a plane one last time. We went to bed with no money in our bank account and woke up able to fly back to Uganda. I have seen God's favor here on this earth, and it is humbling.

A few weeks later, Dustin and I boarded a plane out of Uganda with the twins in tow, about to embark on the longest and hardest three flights of our lives. I swear we almost lost our salvation during those twenty-four hours of travel. We whisper yelled so hard at each other and gave each other enough glares of death to last a solid lifetime. When we landed in Nashville, we gave each other a high five as we exited the plane and Dustin said, "I'm sorry for the things I said to you."

We didn't have anyone meet us at the airport this time. We were exhausted, the twins were a hot mess, and I was honest to God afraid Wyatt was going to burst into tears when he saw them. Wyatt cried for weeks after we got home from our last trip because he only wanted one of the twins to come to live with him, not both. Most days he didn't want either one of them to come live with him. I cried the whole way home from the airport thinking we were about to ruin our family. Ruin Wyatt. Knowing somewhere deep, deep down that we really weren't, but almost mourning the loss of the Original Three and how we had worked so hard to create that sweet life with Wyatt. I cried because I knew we were about to re-enter the war zone that is life after the airport. I was bracing myself for the trenches.

For as many times as I thought we'd never get to this point, we had arrived. We made it. There were officially two more Koctars residing under our roof. It was a joy to introduce the world to the twins, Anita and Kakuru, they were almost three and a few days younger than Wyatt. People would ask us frequently if we did that on purpose. No, we did not mean for that to happen. But we had basically three-year-old triplets. Parties of five were the most fabulous parties ever, or so I heard.

My mom and sister brought Wyatt over the following morning. We met them out in the front yard and I watched anxiously as all of my children met again on U.S. soil. I pointed to Wyatt and said his name to the twins. They rattled off something we didn't understand. My mom had taken Wyatt shopping while we were gone, and he handed each of his siblings a new matchbox car. He looked skeptical, unsure, I felt the same way. We gathered on the front porch and my mom took a picture; our first picture as a family of five. We said our goodbyes, turned around and walked inside all together. Let the work begin.

Those first few weeks are a total blur. I honestly cannot account for most of it. I washed so many loads of laundry only to come back to it days later having to re-wash it. Apparently, you have to remember to switch laundry over for it to dry. A lot of days I got to dinner and thought, "I don't remember if I ate lunch today." I unloaded dishes only to remember I never ran the dishwasher. We survived on more coffee and grace than I knew possible.

We spent the majority of our days breaking up fights because our kids didn't like each other. I was hoping one day they would, but right then they didn't. That's the truth. When you've only ever survived, learning you don't have to anymore is one of the world's hardest lessons. We don't spit on people when they make us mad. We don't choke people because they looked at you the wrong way because that could kill them. We don't scratch a person like a feral cat when they play with something we touched yesterday. Learning how to share when you've never had anything to share before is laugh out loud excruciating. They were learning how to act like humans, and it was painful. I told kids to stop licking walls, chewing on blinds and trying to rip out the outlet protectors. Light switches were completely broken because when you've never seen electricity before obsessively turning on and off the lights all day long makes sense. Books were consumed, and toys were destroyed with teeth. We were knee deep in teaching our kids what to do with basic items because they genuinely didn't know.

They didn't know what to do with a book because they never really had books before. They didn't know what to do with dolls or cars. They didn't know what a swing or a trampoline was. They didn't know what a slide was because they had never been to a playground before. We were drowning as we taught our kids how to play and take care of things because they didn't know how. They didn't know because they never had anything before.

Everything was new and different and terrifying. For the longest time they were petrified of my iPhone. Every time we tried to Facetime someone at least one of the twins would run away screaming. The computer was the same way. Every noise or sound they heard was something they most likely had never heard before and it was panic inducing. The lawnmower going next door, the ding of the doorbell or the grind of the blender could send everyone into a state of pandemonium. I cursed all trains and airplanes for a very long time.

We spent hours on hours, so many hours, listening to one of our children tantrum. Grief is a jerk and rage was the current answer. The twins' lives were flipped upside down and set on fire, and that was, only a little bit, confusing for the almost three-year-old brain to handle. Rules when you've never had them? Consequences? Structure and boundaries and expectations when you've only ever done what you wanted and when you wanted to do it? And all of these things were being asked in a language they didn't understand. We couldn't communicate with each other. I knew what I wanted to tell them, but they couldn't understand. They knew what they wanted to tell me, but I couldn't understand them. The tension right there was so thick it was basically boiling over. Changing cultures is impossibly hard. Being ripped away from the only place you've ever known and thrown into a new world is not for the faint of heart. Being stripped of your language and asked to learn a new one is so mean, it's necessary, but it's also so mean. Learning to live in a family does not happen overnight.

They were learning so many things I didn't know how to teach. We were learning how to trust each other. They were learning what a mom is and what a dad is. They were learning they didn't belong to every white person they saw because when you've never belonged with anyone before that is a complicated lesson to learn.

They were learning how to love- we were learning all over again that showing love with words and actions often precedes the feeling of love and that's okay. We were learning how to parent children who did not love us right then. They didn't love us because they didn't know us. They didn't love us because they didn't know what love was. We were sloshing through the dark waters of learning how to be a family. Strangers don't just magically become a family overnight. Turning strangers into family might be the greatest work of my life.

We now had two children who were learning what it was like to always have enough food. They were learning they didn't have to eat out of the trash can anymore. We had kids eat so much food in one sitting they pooped their pants because the body can only physically take in so much in one sitting. They were learning they didn't have to do that anymore. They were learning what it's like to feel full. When you've never been full, or you've only ever been hungry your brain doesn't know what to do with the opposite all of a sudden. We had two children who had only ever been on a soft food diet, so they were learning how to chew. If you've never tried to teach a three-year-old who doesn't understand you how to chew it's stupid. They were learning, like infants, how to handle different textures of food. There was so much gagging and choking and throwing up going on.

They were learning what it was like to have their needs met by the same two people always. They were learning what it was like to have one mom and one dad. They were learning that family can be safe. They were learning how to ask for help because someone will help you. They were learning that it was okay to fall and get hurt because someone will come to pick you up and put a band-aid on. They were learning they could receive affection because this kind of affection was good, okay and safe. We now had two children who were learning what authority looked like- that it's okay to be told no- you can throw a hot, raging poop yourself tantrum about it for however long you wanted to, and the answer was still the same. We would still be right here, probably somewhat frazzled but we would still be right there. We had two learning about the art of forever. We are not going anywhere; we're yours forever.

We were an awkward group of strangers forced into this role of family, and we were all just learning day by day how to be one. Adoption has taught that you don't become a family magically overnight, but you genuinely grow into one over time. Growing into one can be painful, and it can take a long, long time, but it is possible.

I was not convinced yet we would all survive this but in the same breath I was so, so proud of all three of my children. They walked right into this life so gracefully I could have cried. They were different people than the ones I lived with in Uganda all those months ago. Exactly none of them chose this for a life, but I will be eternally grateful this life picked them. I was rooting so hard for those three. Family looked good on them.

18

THREE, THREE-YEAR-OLDS

I don't know how the average family transitions up in their number of children, but we essentially went from a precious family of three frolicking through fields of sunflowers to parenting three dinosaurs who were trying to eat us overnight. It felt hostile. Something I would like to discuss openly is the three-year-old. No one tells you about them, or at least no one was brave enough to let me in on the secret. I heard all about the "terrible two's" but three, my God, laughs in the face of the two-year-old. And maybe I'm being dramatic and maybe one three year old is fine, but all I know is I lived for one full calendar year with three three- year-olds, and I am almost dead.

Whoever invented the phrase "terrible twos" should be

immediately fired from their job because contrary to popular belief it is not a thing. I feel incredulous over this. If you thought two was terrible, and I thought it was pretty insane, brace yourself, sister. I want to go back and pat Dustin and me on the head when we were exactly like, "Three three-year-olds? Sounds crazy for sure but at least we'd be done with the twos." We were so precious.

In my opinion, the two-year-old doesn't give a damn; and the three-year-old is a walking, talking middle finger. I stand by these observations. They are so mean and irrational. The three-year-old will light your house on fire and straight up walk away just because you had the audacity to look in their direction wrong. They are potential terrorists, and we do not negotiate with terrorists. I don't know what the most vicious animal on earth is but three-year-olds are whatever animal that is. They're monsters. We love them dearly, but they are monsters.

Whenever we were dumb enough to leave the confines of our home and venture out in public with our circus people would casually ask, "So what's it really like?" as if all of this was some sort of mystery when in reality if you just hung around long enough you'd see for yourself what it was really like. Oh, look, someone put a knife in your leg while you closed your eyelids in order to restore moisture to your eyeballs. Also, one of your children is lost, and the other one is eating snacks out of a stranger's purse. See?

I do not condone violence but having three three-year-olds was basically like managing a three-year-old fight club. The same rules which applied to Brad Pitt applied to my children. I felt less like a civilized mother and more like a bouncer who was also really great at getting snacks.

1st RULE: You do not talk about FIGHT CLUB.

2nd RULE: You DO NOT talk about FIGHT CLUB.

3rd RULE: If someone says, "stop" or goes limp, taps out the fight is over.

4th RULE: Only two guys to a fight.

5th RULE: One fight at a time.

6th RULE: No shirts, no shoes.

7TH RULE: Fights will go on as long as they have to.

8th RULE: If this is your first night of FIGHT CLUB, you HAVE to fight.

I mentioned the twins did not come into our family speaking or understanding English, right? It was mostly fine. In one morning alone Anita thought George Washington, Hillary Clinton, and some random white child on the television were all her grandmother. She called me baby for a very long time. Every last thing was a ball. I had kids pointing at lights and calling them cars. They would point to their belly buttons and call them rice. The twins very regularly called me daddy. We had a list of words written in their native language, and you could find us saying things like, "You need to tula* in your chair right now" and "Do you need to fuka*? No? What about pama*?" I could minutely be found shouting "GABA!! We gaba* our toys!" At bedtime, I would whisper until I was blue in the face, "Go to webake*. No, you may not get up right now. It is time for webake*. You have to lie down and go to webake*. GO TO WEBAKE*." They didn't have one clue what I was saying to them, and we didn't have one clue what they were saying to us. It felt very much like the definition of a hot mess.

For almost a full year all three of our children were in diapers. Like, real diapers we threw away in the trash can. We were changing something like one hundred diapers a week. If some study comes out revealing the environment took a turn for the worse during the years 2016-2017 is was single-handed because of us. I will own it. Do not even come at me with the fact that most kids are toilet trained by the time they are three. Mine were not. Primarily because two out of three had never seen a toilet before and were utterly petrified by the white fixture they were being asked to sit on and do their business. But also because once we got over that fear, I would frequently find a child sitting on the piece of hardware in the bathroom spread eagle.

I cannot fully explain the number of times I looked up to find someone *missing* in our home. If we were to live in a mansion this would make sense to my brain but our house is small, so it seemed complicated for me to make sense of at the time. I would often walk into a room and exclaim:

Why are you licking the door!?

Why have all of the air vents been ripped up out of the floor!?

Why are their nails in your mouth!?

Why is your diaper off!?

IS THAT POOP!?

You cannot run away!

Why do you have a knife!?

Why is the bath running!?

How did you take all the art off the wall?!

Why are you ripping apart a baby doll!?

Why are you up there!?

How did you climb up the actual wall!?

Why are you acting like the TV is a punching bag!?

Why are you trying to stick something pointy in the electrical outlet!?

Why am I standing in pee!?

My favorite part of the day was the times we had to consume nutrients. This is also what civilians refer to as meal time. I'd say most small children are dramatic tyrants during the meal time hours, but this was on another level. Someone was always choking or gagging or throwing up or throwing food or spitting something out or asking for more or saying they didn't like it. Someone was quite literally always crying. Passive aggressive temper tantrums were thrown throughout each meal. My kitchen looked as if we should have burned it down. Mealtime with three feral toddlers is not on my list of favorite past times.

Somehow we always made it through each entire day and had to put all of these people to bed some kind of way. My mom liked to encourage me by saying all of her children were great sleepers which surprisingly was not all that encouraging because precisely zero of my children had ever heard of sleep before. No one was ever in their bed, and at most times both an adult and a child could be found crying in the dark. Every night Dustin and I gave each the Mockingbird Hand Signal only hoping we would see each other on the other side. One night after dinner this conversation went down in our kitchen:

Me: How do you want to do this?

Dustin: I don't want to put the twins to bed.

Me: I don't want to get up in the middle of the night.

Dustin: Deal.

Me: Deal.

And then we would get up and do it all over again the next day. It felt like a really twisted version of Groundhog Day. We can mostly laugh about it now years removed. Only mostly. So when people used to ask, "What's it really like?" or "What do your days look like?" I would find myself unable to control my face as I said, "Look, we're just trying to make sure every single one of us is alive, and our house hasn't burned to the ground by the end of the day."

True story.

THE END.

*Tula= sit

*Fuka= pee

*Pama= poop

*Gaba= share

*Webake= sleep

19

A DAY IN THE LIFE

4:30 am: Child #2 wakes up and screams like a dinosaur

4:31 am: All three children stand in our room crying

4:32 am: Change diapers and usher small, crying children to the playroom

4:33 am- 5:30 am: Pour coffee; break up a fight that resulted in blood; console bleeding, screaming child; try to console and correct The Attacker, The Attacker does not speak English; attempt to make breakfast; break up another fight; put toys children are fighting over in time-out; all three children stand at my feet screaming; child #2 spits on child #1, try talking to child #2 but child #2 doesn't speak English, all three children continue to stand at my feet screaming; silently sob over poured bowls of cereal, child #3 hits child #1; console child #1; try talking to child #3 but child #3 does not speak English; child #1 asks if today is the day we get to take child #2 and child #3 back to Uganda; child #1 cries loudly when I say, "no"; usher small, crying children to the table for breakfast

5:30 am- 7:30 am: Child #2 continues to cry loudly; attempt to help child #2 calm down and eat but child #2 spits on me; child #3 gags; attempt to correct behavior, but child #2 does not speak English; child #3 gags more; child #3 chokes; child #2 is now screaming and banging fists on table; child #3 almost pukes; attempt to calm child #2 but child #2 doesn't speak English; inform child #2 that if they continue to scream and hit the table they will go sit on their bed; child #1 asks for more food; child #2 continues screaming and throws food across the kitchen; remove child #2 from the table, escort them to their bed and inform them whenever they are done screaming they can come back to the table; child #3 asks for more food; child #2 continues to scream; Dustin leaves for work; child #3 chokes, child #3 starts crying, ask child #3 what is wrong but child #3 does not speak English; child #1 goes to play, starts crying because child #2 broke another toy; go calm down child #2 successfully, escort them back to the table to eat breakfast; child #2 refuses to eat breakfast and stares at me for 45 minutes; child #2 finishes breakfast

7:32 am: Make all children sit on the couch and turn on the TV

7:35 am: Reheat cup of coffee, try to clean up the kitchen

7:35am- 8:30 am: Go back and forth from the kitchen to the couch because all children are screaming that another child is touching them

8:34 am: Change diapers

8:35 am: Child #3 poops

8:36 am: Child #1 asks for a snack

8:36 am-9:30 am: Prepare snack, convince children to eat snack, child #3 gags, child #2 chokes, child #1 asks what we are doing today, clean up semi-uneaten snack

9:31am: Child #1 poops

9:35 am: Child #2 poops

9:40 am- 11:00 am: Tell children we are going to the park; child #1 cries because they do not want to go to the park; change my clothes; child #2 eats a book; child #3 is eating out of the trashcan; child #2 destroys a toy with their teeth; child #1 weeps; child #3 bites child #1, child #1 pushes child #2, child #2 scratches child #1; all three children stand at my feet screaming; change child #1's clothes; child #2 tries to strangle child #1; child #1 cannot breath momentarily; child #3 poops; change diaper; change child #2's clothes; child #3 removes diaper and pees on floor; clean up floor; child #1 asks for a snack; find child #2 chewing on the blinds in the kitchen; child #3 turns on the bath; child #2 rips pillow apart with bare hands; take pillow away and correct child #2 but child #2 does not speak English; child #2 throws themselves on the floor, wailing; clean up stuffing; child #2 poops themselves while screaming; change diaper; child #2 kicks me in the face; child #3 asks for a snack; change child #3's clothes

11:01am- 11:30am: Put child #1's shoes on; put child #2's shoes on; put child #3's shoes on; child #2 removes shoes; child

#2 head butt's me when I try to put their shoes back on; child #2 throws body onto ground weeping and thrashing violently; child #1 pushes child #3, child #3 bites child #1; all three children are howling; forcibly put on child #2's shoes

11:31am: Realize its lunch time, say a few curse words out loud

11:32am-12:30 pm: Prepare lunch; bribe children to eat lunch; child #3 gags; child #2 chokes; child #1 asks for more; child #2 refuses to eat; child #3 refuses to eat; bribe children with candy; clean up lunch

12:30pm- 2:00 pm: Change diapers; lay all children down on separate parts of the couch for nap time; pat child #2's back until they fall asleep; pat child #1's back until they fall asleep; pat child #3's back until they fall asleep; realize I haven't eaten or been to the bathroom today; child #2 wakes us; child #1 wakes up; child #3 wakes up

2:05 pm: Change diapers

2:30 pm: Arrive at park

2:32 pm: Child #1 runs off to play; child #3 walks up to every woman and calls them "mommy"; child #2 eats mulch; child #1 finds a "magic stick" and tries to make child #2 and child #3 disappear, violently sobs when it doesn't work; child #3 tries to snuggle with a stranger; child #2 thrashes and weeps on the ground because a swing they were swinging on twelve minutes ago is now in use by someone else; child #1 poops; walk all the children back to the car to change diaper; walk back to the playground; child #3 tells another stranger they love them; child #3 tries to go home with a different stranger; airplane flies by, terrified child #2 falls on the ground weeping; child #1 asks for a snack; child #3 eats a stranger's snack; child #2 is inconsolable on ground; child #3 poops; tell kids we are leaving the park; child #1 runs to the left, child #2 snaps out of it and runs off to the right, poopy child #3 sits down on the ground at my feet; wrangle all children to the car

4:00pm: Arrive home

4:05pm: Child #2 kicks child #1 in the face, child #1 shoves child #2 into a wall; child #3 is found playing with a knife; child #2 stands on the top of a chair and takes pictures off of the walls; child #2 picks paint off the wall and eats it; child #3 break a light switch; child #1 asks for a snack; child #2 and child #3 start crying, ask what is wrong but they can't speak English; child #1 wants me to read a book; child #1 wants me to roll cars; child #1 wants to do a puzzle; child #2 and child #3 are still howling

5:15pm: Dustin arrives home, plays with children while I make something for dinner; child #2 screams incessantly

5:45 pm: Usher hungry, angry, whiny children to the table for dinner

5:46pm- 6:45 pm: Child #2 eats entire plate of food in four minutes, asks for more; child #3 gags, chokes, almost throws ups; child #1 doesn't like what's for dinner; child #2 eats entire second plate of dinner in six minutes, asks for more; child #3 chokes; child #2 eats entire third plate of dinner in three minutes, asks for more, wails when we say "no"; child #2 poops; child #3 starts crying

7:00pm: Change diapers; put on pajamas; I put child #1 to bed, they ask if tomorrow will be the day we take child #2 and child #3 back to Uganda, cries when I say "probably not;" Dustin sits in child #2 and child #3's bedroom until they fall asleep

8:00pm: We meet up in the kitchen, Dustin asks how the day was, I cry into his chest while recounting the day; eat a cracker for dinner

8:30pm: Crawl in bed with my clothes on

1:15am: Child #1 wakes up crying, go get them back to sleep

2:00 am: Child #2 wakes up crying, go get them back to sleep

3:23 am: Child #3 wakes up crying, go get them back to sleep

4:30am: Child #2 wakes up and screams like a dinosaur

4:31 am: All three children stand in our room crying

20

LOVE CAN LIVE HERE

When I woke up in the mornings all I felt was seething anger. I felt regret. I was sad. I screamed into my pillow some mornings and other mornings I sobbed into it. Our life felt ugly, dark; people didn't understand. I hate the people who believe adoption stops at the airport. The people who believe once a child is in your home it is good, that it makes sense, that it is easy. Those people wouldn't have touched my life with a four hundred foot pole. Adoption does not stop at the airport; it begins there. We had stepped into a war zone, there are bombs everywhere, and you couldn't see them. You only notice them when you step on one, and it blows your leg right off your body. It's called the trenches for a reason.

I want to like them, I want to love them, but I don't. All I felt was dislike, and sometimes I felt a deep seeded hatred that scared me to death. Life had suddenly separated itself; life before the twins and life after the twins. Sometimes I missed my life before. I felt shame; I was disgusted with myself for these feelings. I felt embarrassed and guilty by this admission. "You felt this way with Wyatt," Dustin reminded me. "It took you a long time to like and feel love for him," and he was right. I had felt the same way in the beginning with Wyatt, but this also felt different. It felt bigger, scarier, and I couldn't explain why.

I was reminded of something my counselor told me about giving birth. She explained how hormones and endorphins are released during labor that make you feel happy and in love. This is on purpose; it was God's design to connect a mother with her baby. There were no hormones released when I was handed my children. There were no endorphins sent to my brain to help my heart.

I was presented with this idea of cups, that when I was handed each one of my children I was also handed a cup with their name on it. Over time I fill that cup with positive memories or funny stories or things I like about a child. The cup is there so I have something to pull from when things are tough. It's there to remind me of whom my child is, who is behind the behavior. Except some of my cups were empty, I had years to fill Wyatt's cup up, and I had done that. His cup was filled to the brim because I had time to fill it to the brim. I was much more patient with him; every little thing didn't irritate the stew out of me. He was not perfect, no child is, but I was not as nitpicky and overtly critical of him like I was with the other two. Every last thing the twins did drove me bananas, and I couldn't shake it off but the cups made sense to me because the twin's cups were empty. And the only thing you can do with empty cups is allow yourself the time to fill them up; you cannot fast track this step. The twins' cups were empty because we had never spent any time together; they were empty because we didn't know one another. I didn't know who they were or what they were like. I didn't have any positive memories or funny stories, not yet. And so whenever something hard was happening, or they did something frustrating or mean, or I found myself irritated, I had nothing to pull from to remind me of who they really were. Filling up cups takes an exorbitant amount of time. Adoption is not natural, the love I would eventually grow to feel for my children would be a love that was fought for and hard earned.

The twins didn't like me; I could see it in their eyes. They were mean to me; they spit on me and screamed at me and bit me. They were mad at me, and I understood why. I knew this was hard for them; I knew it wasn't fair and didn't make any sense to their brains. The twins didn't need me; they were self-sufficient in a three-year-old way. They didn't want help and would spit in my face when I offered it, but then they would scream at me when I didn't offer to help them the following time. They wanted me to read their minds and were enraged when I couldn't. They didn't want me to meet their needs because they wanted to meet their own needs. They knew what they wanted, what they needed, but they couldn't communicate it to me because we didn't speak the same language.

They didn't want anything to do with me; they didn't want to be held or carried or rocked. They did want those things, but they didn't know how to do them. They didn't know how to be held or how to be carried or how to be rocked. They wanted to snuggle up next to me and sit in my lap, but they couldn't figure out how to do it. They were stiff as boards and uncomfortable after too long. They were mad when I wouldn't let them sit in other people's laps, and they oftentimes refused to sit in mine. They would watch Wyatt's ease at which he received affection and attention, and they couldn't quite figure out how to do the same. We were solely surviving, and this kind of survival didn't look like love. I never knew when the other shoe would drop; I walked around on eggshells.

I ran through the house chasing squealing children. I tickled and peeked around corners saying, "boo!" to shrieks of laughter. They turned around and bolted passed me, running back to the other end of the house. I pretended not to be able to catch them. I tagged one child tickling them, but they accidentally tripped over my feet trying to get away and fell to the ground. I try to help them up but something snaps, I couldn't guess what if my life was on the line. They look up at me as if I am the Devil himself, their eyes are dark and overcome. They spit on me and begin screaming. I offer an apology and try to calm them down even though they are unable to understand the words coming out of my mouth. Before I can decide what to do next the screaming stops, the child storms off and the game goes with them.

We sit down at the kitchen table, and one child won't eat

anything. I ask them to take a bite, and the fuse has been lit. They will flail and thrash and scream with fury for an hour. My jaw clenches and I feel on edge. As soon as it stops the entire house exhales. There is a squabble over a toy, and I say gently something about taking turns and the fuse lights again. Another hour, sometimes two is spent raging with fury. They stare through me with their eyes. I think sometimes their eyes could kill me.

I sit on a child's bed reading books to everyone. They all want to sit in my lap, and so I tell them we will take turns, and we do. Nobody screams at me this time, and I exhale a sigh of relief. They each take a turn picking a book and sitting in my lap as I read it. The twins crawl awkwardly into my lap unsure of how to relax against me; it feels foreign because it is. It feels forced and uncomfortable. I try to situate them, help them out but as soon as I do they bolt out of the room. It was too much. Maybe we'll try again another time.

We are outside playing in the swimming pool I filled up earlier, and two kids begin arguing over some cups. I say something about sharing and attempt to redistribute the cups evenly. Rage comes rushing out of one of my children. It is so forceful and overwhelming. It cannot be contained or calmed down. The other shoe has dropped over sharing cups, and I want to cuss. The screaming doesn't stop for hours. It finally does and as quickly as it stops it begins again over someone touching them. The life feels like it is being sucked out of our home.

They screamed at me for hours on end, day after day and I hated it. I felt it in my bones, this hatred for all the screaming.

Sometimes I looked down, and my hands were shaking. I felt bitter and defeated. My life felt awkward, and I couldn't fix it. Everything felt so hard. It felt like we were suffocating, maybe forcibly being held underwater, or being hit repeatedly by waves unable to catch our footing. It felt like survival by fire.

Love is a choice; I knew this. I had, after all, lived this part before. Love is a verb; it is something you do; it is not always something you feel. Just because you choose the action of love does not mean it will be received and it does not mean it will translate to the feeling of love. Love is not always easy, and it does not always make sense, but love is the right thing to do. I wrote 1 Corinthians 13:4-8 on a post-it note and taped it up on the cabinet above the sink. It was the same verses that had been read at our wedding years before, but this time the verses meant something different. Love was not just patient anymore, patience is a nice idea but this time love was long-suffering. That is what this kind of love felt like to me; a love that would suffer long. I continued to practice the act of love daily, and it continued to be met with spit to my face. This kind of love felt more like a sacrifice; this kind of love felt like commitment at all cost.

"What do you like about them?" a friend asked. It was a good question, one that reframed our circumstances but I couldn't think of anything. I felt like a monster. Later I scrounged up a list, and it was so short it made me laugh and then burst into tears. I didn't want it to be like this.

I sat down on the couch in the middle of my kids as they watched TV. Wyatt leaned his head against my arm, and I didn't think twice about it. It was a simple act, one that had been learned over time and it felt as natural as breathing. I felt like his mom. A few minutes later one of the twins tried the same thing on my other side except it was awkward and forced, and I cringed. I cringed at the touch of one of my children, and I felt devastated by that. I wanted to get up and run away, but love told me to stay. I could do this; I could fall in love with two more children. I sat there planked between two children who called me mommy and it only partially felt right. One half of my body felt relaxed, and the other half felt on fire, I wanted to crawl out of my skin, but we stayed there. Committed to the act of love believing the feeling would follow suit.

Love is an art; it is a practice. Love at its core is a verb. You cannot love someone you do not know, and getting to know people takes time. You cannot force love, and sometimes that is painful. Love can be scary, and there are times it is easier to fight than to love. Sometimes we must try love on for size, take it off and try it on again the following day. Sometimes you must fake it until you make it and you just might not make for a very long time. I grew to love one child, and I believed deep in my bones I could grow to love two more. I believed love could live here.

21

YOU WILL SURVIVE

The first year the twins were in our home I felt like we lived the same day for three hundred and sixty five days. It's mostly a blur to look back on. I can honestly say I don't recall much of my children's third year of life, but I do remember some things like the unexpected goodness of people. God repeatedly winked at me throughout that year through the kindness of others towards us.

For months we didn't buy any diapers; we had the most magnificent diaper fairies on planet earth. Boxes would magically show up on our front porch at the exact time we were running out. We had meals delivered to us for weeks, groceries sent straight to our doorstep, clothes poured in, and a friend sent a cleaning service to clean our house because God is good all the time. People gifted us gift cards for days. People are good I knew this but to experience people's goodness is something no one can ever take away from me. To be the recipient of kindness and generosity and sacrifice is rather holy. People sprinkled kindness on us like it was confetti and it changed me forever.

After we came home with the twins, we traded in both of our cars and bought the treasure that Wyatt now refers to as our "van car." We proceeded to live life with one car, and it turned out to be finer than I thought it would be. We took Dustin to work every morning and picked him up every night. We said no to things we couldn't both do at the same time, and we lived to tell about it. We were saving anything and everything we could so we could purchase a second car when we were able to. We went everywhere or nowhere as a family; it was both awesome and stupid. I remember months before this when I started praying for a car; it felt dumb at first like God was going to drop a car in our laps straight out of heaven just because I was praying for it. But once we knew the twins were going to join our family officially, we knew we were going to have to get a new car, and in life's perfect timing both of our cars needed to be replaced and we couldn't afford to do so, and so I started praying for a car. For so many months I prayed fervently for a vehicle, and we never got a one; it didn't happen, and so I stopped praying for one. One random night after the kids were in bed and we were mindlessly watching TV we got a phone call from someone saying they had been given money by several people who wanted to remain anonymous; these people wanted to do something for us, and so they bought us a second car. It is currently, years later, sitting in my driveway as I type this. Sometimes I am still in disbelief.

We didn't go to church as a family for months. I remember our Pastor's wife asking if I would share our story one Sunday morning not long after the twins were in our home and I couldn't do it. I was so miserable and angry, and everything sucked so hard. I could not stand before the Lord and say any kind words, and so I sent my husband instead; he is the nice one. I remember the Sunday we did decide to grace church with our entire family's presence and it went exactly as I thought it would. We dropped all three kids off in class, and I walked away feeling so relieved, there had been no tears, and I could breathe for a minute. We found our seats and halfway through worship I saw her walking towards us, and I knew; she leaned in and whispered, "Does Kakuru call you mommy? We have tried to calm him down, but he is screaming for mommy." I will never get over the fact that she had the awareness to ask me if my son called me mommy.

One morning I asked my mom to come over and watch all three kids while I went to the dentist. I had missed an entire year's worth of scheduled and re-scheduled appointments. Between going back and forth to Uganda, taking kids to their own appointments, retrieving endless amounts of snacks, breaking up fights, and walking around like a general zombie I had failed to find time for things like dental hygiene; that felt so minor on a Tuesday compared to everything else. But I made it to the dentist that morning and was called back and laid down in my chair. The sheer act of sitting down with not one hand touching me or asking me for anything made me want to weep for joy. I made small talk with the woman cleaning my teeth, and when she asked what I did for a living, I replied, "Oh I stay at home with our three kids." "You have the hardest job of all," she immediately replied. We got to talking about each of our families and when I relayed the facts of having three three-year-olds she looked at me and said, "Oh bless your heart. I remember those days. Lie down, I'm going to turn on HGTV, and I promise I'll take at least an hour on your teeth. If I'm done before my next appointment, you can lie here and watch TV." Then she did exactly that; she let me lie in a chair for over an hour, and she didn't ask any more questions. She cleaned my teeth in silence and did not require me to move one muscle; I felt like a queen. She apologized for making me leave and said, "I'm proud of you for getting here; moms are always last on the list. And you know what? I'm not even going to tell you to floss. You're just doing a good job." I have tears in my eyes as I recount these stories.

During easily one of my worst parenting days of all times, I hit a car in a parking lot in a sequence of events I will tell no one ever. It was mortifying. I thought for sure I was going to be on the news because of this ridiculous parking lot incident. I didn't go back to this parking lot for an entire year. I called my mom in a straight panic and followed that up with a phone call to Dustin where I uttered, "I need to tell you something. Do not be a jerk." Marriage is fun.

I waited around for a while for the owner of the car to come back. All three kids were sweating, hungry, crying, and angry. I didn't know if it could get any worse than this, but then I saw a black woman storming towards us with an incredulous look on her face. I usually do not point out a person's race when it is irrelevant to the story, but her race mattered that day; I believe it in my bones. I watched her look at the damage done to her car and look at me; then her eyes moved to the open van door. She looked at my kids, kind of tilted her head, looked back at me and immediate favor came over her face. I cannot explain it. I took a deep breath, walked over and attempted to explain what happened. Living an embarrassing story is one thing but then having to use words and tell it is another. I apologized profusely. She looked at me and said, "It is okay. It really is. It's just a car. Thank goodness no one was hurt. You know with everything going on in the world today I think we need to be more kind to each other." Tears formed in my eyes immediately. She then said, "You call your husband and tell him you hit a car, and the lady is not mad about it and to get over it. Husbands can sometimes just make things worse." We exchanged information, and she gave me a big hug. She peeked into our car and talked to each one of my children. We said "Goodbye," and both went on with our days.

That afternoon I called our insurance company and took the car to the shop so everything could be fixed. I didn't end up on the news like I thought I would. Life continued moving forward, and I forgot about it. A couple of months later, Dustin handed me an envelope with my name on it, and when I read the words written in cursive, I laughed out loud. It was a thank you note from Ms. P; for not driving away when I could have. The whole thing is still absurd and perfect. Her card sits in my Bible to this day. People are kind and good; love always wins.

One morning I wrestled all three kids out the door after a hard morning and let them all lose on a hiking trail. They ran ahead of me while I inhaled the fresh air and prayed we'd make it through the day. A woman stopped us and asked the million dollar question, "Are they triplets?" She proceeded to tell me she had twins who were grown now. She looked me square in the eyes and said, "This is the hardest thing you will ever do. It is so hard. I remember. You will survive this. They will survive this. Just show up. Don't worry about being present right now just feed them and love them. They will grow up. They aren't going to kill each other even when you think they really might. Even though this is crazy right now, I promise you will all look back on this time with fondness."

It's always the little things when you're in the middle of an overwhelming season. It's the meal that is dropped off on the perfect day or the person who returns your shopping cart at the store because they see you wrestling multiple small humans and groceries into your car all at once. It's free babysitting so you can go eat food and speak grown-up words to your husband. It's the bottle of wine on your doorstep with the card attached which reads, "You're doing a great job!" It's the person who decides to pay for your meals when they have no idea finances are tight. It's the seasoned mother who speaks not words of, "You'll miss this one day!" but rather words of life, "This is hard! They will grow up! You will be okay!"

Even though I didn't believe her that day while hiking with my children, it turns out she was correct. We would, in fact, survive every single day and live to tell about it. My children have yet to kill each, and I feel hopeful, positive, we will one day look back on their childhood years with fondness. There is at least a decent amount of video footage of laughter and good times had by all.

22

SOMETIMES I LOVE YOU

For months every single morning, Wyatt would ask, "Is today the day we get to take brother and sister back to Uganda?" I would listen to him wail after I replied in the negative. Every night as I tucked him into bed he would whisper, "Is tomorrow the day we get to take brother and sister back to Uganda?" I would rub his back and sing while he cried himself to sleep most nights. I will never get over how much all three of my children hated each other in the beginning. I begged God to do work only he could do and watched him do it over month's right before me.

One night I had curry simmering on the stove, and a glass of wine had been poured. My back door was open while the kids ran inside and back outside squealing with delight. Anita was sticking her baby doll in her shirt, carrying her around and finding places for her to sleep. The boys were riding bikes and laughing, arguing and playing with their cars, and trying to wake up their sister's baby much to her frustration and laughing some more. I stirred the curry and took every ounce of it in; we were going to be okay.

A few weeks prior we had gone over to a friend's house to play. We did something as simple as sit in another room while all our kids ate lunch together and it felt like we had summited Mt. Everest. It hit me like a ton of bricks; I couldn't have done that before then because the twins would not have trusted I would exit a room and come back for them. Before the twins didn't know how to sit at a table or use a utensil and that day they did both. Earlier one of my kids would have been standing in the corner scratching paint off the wall and eating it; and then would have thrown a raging tantrum for the next several hours because we do not do that. That day no tantrums were thrown, and they sat and used a fork and said excuse me. My people mostly shared and played with toys the way they were supposed to be played with. No one physically hurt another human being on purpose that day.

Not long before then the twins would have called my friend mommy because they didn't know what that word meant. They would have wanted to stay at my friend's house not because it's not normal to want to stay where your friends and fun things are, but because they didn't understand they belonged with us. But, my God, if you had peeked into my friend's house that day, you wouldn't have been able to tell who was new here and still trying to figure out America, family, trust, forever or life as we know it. It was a beautiful, holy moment for me.

The twins had been stateside for almost six months and life had softened a bit. We stood outside one night after dinner watching our kids trying to catch lightning bugs when Dustin leaned over and said, "This life is fun sometimes." I caught myself off guard with, "I know. I think I'm starting to kind of like it." Enduring a terrible season is just that, surviving a terrible season, one you couldn't pretend was fun even if you were given a lifetime of free Chick-Fil-A. You put your head down and do it. Then you get to sometimes. You can breathe a little bit, and you don't hate everyone always. The tantrums have died down some and people have stopped consuming books. You don't feel like you're physically going to die anymore and you're starting to laugh again genuinely. It feels like a little, tiny gift or magic or maybe a miracle; entirely possible all of the above.

I remember so distinctly the day my kids first said I love you to one another. We were back hiking our favorite trail not too far from our house when we stopped at the spot by the lake to throw rocks in. Many a rock has been thrown into this lake by our family; it's therapeutic, the act of throwing rocks. I stood there watching as one by one each child would pick up a rock and chuck it across the lake. They all three stood with their backs to me in a row when I overheard Wyatt say, "I love you, Anita. I love you, Kakuru." He paused and then let out, "Well, sometimes I love you and sometimes I don't." We might make it after all.

Often I would find myself sitting around marveling at how far we had all come. Those days were far from perfect and most days didn't even feel remotely good. But then I would find myself sitting on the floor in a dark kitchen at the end of the day after everyone had been tucked in bed and was fast asleep and remember there had been laughter, hugs, popcorn, movies, and dance parties in the car. There had been happy moments. I ended every day hugging and kissing everyone goodnight. Most days Wyatt would whisper into my ear, "I'm glad you're here, mommy." Those days were so far from being perfect, but those days were enough. His mercies proved to be true each and every morning, glory be.

23

THE DOG DAYS OF MOTHERHOOD

I found myself soaking wet in anger early on. With every wipe of a nose and kiss of a boo-boo and change of a diaper, I felt it crawling around. With every call of my name and every mess cleaned up and every broken up fight, it was right there under the surface. With every tantrum thrown and ugly word spewed to my face, it threatened to boil over. With every challenging behavior and slap to my face and refusal to go to sleep, it whispered in my ear. With every meal made and every snack gotten and every cup of water or milk or lemonade poured, there it was. Anger was the friend I didn't want hanging around, and yet there it always was.

I texted my mom one morning and asked if she could watch my kids so I could go away for a minute. We were in the car as soon as she replied, "yes." I drove to the park down the street from where I grew up and ran the same six-mile loop I have run probably hundreds of times. It's the loop I ran over and over in high school as I battled an eating disorder, and it's the loop I ran when Dustin and I fought over some wedding related nonsense. It's the loop I run when I am training for a race, and it's the same loop I run to make sure I've still got it. That six-mile loop holds a lot of blood, sweat, and tears for me. I went and I pounded out those six miles full of fury; like the pavement itself had wronged me. With every step taken and mile run, I let go of the things that had taken up residence inside of my heart.

I'm tired. I'm so freaking tired. I don't want to be touched all day. I feel lonely sometimes. I have terrific friends and a great husband and a beautiful family. It's weird to feel alone in the midst of all of that. I don't feel fulfilled by my kids. I don't feel satisfied by motherhood. Staying at home with my kids is hard. I don't think I'm supposed to go back to work. Being a mom isn't what I thought it would be. Being a mom isn't exactly what I wanted it to be. Why does everyone keep telling me that I'm going to miss having toddlers? I don't really like toddlers all that much; especially not three of them at one time. What if I miss this season as everyone says but what if I don't? Then what? What am I even doing with my life?

I feel bored. I'm never alone. I want to be alone sometimes. I miss being in my house by myself. I wish I weren't wired as an introvert. I wish I were more patient. I hate it that I yell sometimes. I feel like I'm suffocating under all of my kid's needs. This is overwhelming. I don't have anything to talk about anymore. I chose this. Being a mom is hard. Three is a hard age. Three is a hard number. Three kids the same age is insane. Not being able to

*communicate with the twins is awful. Co-parenting has to be the hardest thing
this world will ever ask of us.*

As I said things, I had kept bottled up tight for months because
the world tells you it's best to keep stuff like that a secret, my anger
began to soften. As I acknowledged things I thought were
forbidden to feel I felt lighter. As I said things out loud I had only
ever shoved down deeper I started to feel some light. The more I
stopped pretending everything was fine, the less the darkness
threatened to overcome. Sometimes refusing to acknowledge the
darkness makes trying to find some light feel fake, but the truth
always sets us free.

This really wasn't about my kids; I was growing to like them.
This wasn't about my life; this was a season that would end
whether I wanted it to or not. This wasn't even entirely about my
anger, reigning in a temper is holy, hard, necessary work. This was
about me and my feelings of unworthiness. It was about my
hustling to feel worth doing the dirty work of switching over the
billionth load of laundry or putting away the dishes that never end
or sitting with that child who needed to be sat with. It was about
me trying to feel satisfied doing the secret work of calming down
yet another meltdown or wiping another snotty nose or drinking
one more pretend cup of coffee a child made for me. It was about
me wanting to feel seen when in reality the majority of my days
would go completely unseen. It was about my wanting to feel
fulfilled by anything or anyone other than the person who was
created to fulfill me.

I realized I had put an insane amount of pressure on this act of motherhood. While motherhood can please us and bring an immense amount of joy; it was not meant to satisfy us to our core. My children were not designed to fulfill the deepest parts of me. Just as my spouse does not truly complete me or fill the void and empty spaces within my heart, neither do my kids. It turns out that kind of pressure is anger inducing. That is the kind of pressure that sucks the life out of souls.

God met me right there on the pavement that day. He laced up his Nikes and pounded every mile of that loop right alongside me, and he said, "I see you." He whispered to my soul not words of guilt or shame or anger but words of life and hope and promises. He reminded me that when I feel small and insignificant and unimportant that he notices me. He told me he cheers for me; he believes in me and he was proud of me. He wasn't embarrassed by my flaws. He convinced me that he who began a good work in and through me would finish it to completion. He would not leave me. He would run the race set before me right alongside me. He would not leave me to be eaten by toddlers.

He gets it. He created motherhood. He knows tired. He was touched all day long by people expecting something from him. There were days he didn't get to eat. He was misunderstood. He said the same things over and over again to people who did not get it. I bet in the midst of having his friends he often felt lonely. He was stretched and needed. His life was on purpose, and I believe he was calling me to live like mine was, too.

No one sees me in the kitchen having dance parties just trying to make it through the witching hour. No one hears the conversations about everything and nothing in the dark while tucking little people into bed. No one is clapping for me as I make one more creative dinner people will whine about or read one more book or play one more game of Candy Land. No one sees how many rounds of hide and seek are played in any given day. No one sees me doing the work of taming my temper and running at 5 AM because that's the only way I can do it. No one sees me apologizing to and crying over and praying for these pieces of my heart that walk around outside of my body. No one sees the laughing and chasing and falling into bed exhausted and full to the brim.

But he does. He is convincing me that he is in my corner cheering as I do the work of loving my family to the best of my ability. He is with me in the minutes and on the days that go entirely unnoticed. He is with me when I mess up, and he is with me when I succeed. He is there to pick me right up off the ground when I can't seem to carry on. He is whispering in my ears, "I see you, and I am pleased. Keep pressing on." He is winking at me at every turn. It turns out it just might be a little audacious to carry on with my one wild and precious life believing in a God who sees and is satisfied.

Becoming a mom has been kind of like breaking in a new pair of shoes for me. I'm not a lover of shopping, and I don't have a closet full of shoes for every outfit, but I have bought new shoes in my lifetime, and I usually hate them at first. I love them in the store; they're cute, and they feel good on my feet, and they make me look good in the mirror. But getting home and having to break them in is another story. Every pair of shoes I have ever bought feels weird at first. They're too tight around my toes, my feet can't breathe, and they feel like they're being pinched to death. I always get blisters on my heels. With every new pair of shoes, I have to figure out how it feels to walk in them. I have to learn the bounce of a new pair of running shoes and learn the feel of a new pair of sandals. On the rare occasion, I must figure out how to walk like a human in a new pair of heels. Some shoes I have to stretch out and simply endure the painful stretch of time until the shoes actually fit my feet. Most of the times I consider taking them back to the store at least once because I think I bought the wrong shoes. It always takes a minute until the shoes conform to the shape of my feet and my feet feel comfortable in them. Breaking in motherhood has felt much the same way.

A few years ago I wasn't entirely convinced I was supposed to be a mom. I thought the world had quite possibly made a great mistake. It didn't feel like it fit me. Motherhood didn't feel right to me in the beginning. Everything about it felt fake and forced; it all really hurt, and at times I felt like I was suffocating. I didn't feel very good at it. I didn't trust myself. I didn't know how to walk in this new role I suddenly found myself in. I was sure the outside world thought motherhood looked on me the way it felt on me... unnatural.

Four years ago when I was handed my first born son, I believed I would become a mom right there on the spot. And to some degree I did. I quite literally became a mom standing right there in the scorching heat of Uganda. But what I have learned is that becoming a mom is just that, becoming a mom. To become something is to change or grow into something else. Becoming is a work of art. Caterpillars become butterflies. Cucumbers become pickles. Grapes become wine. Apples become applesauce. Women become mothers. None of these things happen magically overnight with a poof from a magic fairy wand. Instead, caterpillars hang upside down; spin themselves a cocoon and weeks later emerge as a butterfly. Cucumbers sit for days in vinegar and turn into pickles. Grapes take months and sometimes years to become that bottle of wine you enjoy. Apples have to be peeled, cut into, boiled and mashed before they ever turn into applesauce. Women gradually, overtime turn themselves right into mothers.

I didn't know back then that I, too, would have to do the beautiful and painful work of becoming. I didn't know then what becoming would look like. I didn't know then what becoming would feel like. I didn't know at the time it would hurt and humble me and be the most beautiful thing I'd ever do. Because when you're drowning in sleepless nights and blow out diapers and all that crying it's hard to see if you're becoming anything at all other than insane. When you're in the middle of the chaos and confusion and you feel like all you do is step on matchbox cars and curse under your breath, it's easy to think you aren't doing anything at all. When you can't see past all the bickering and arguing and complaining it's hard to tell if your work here matters. But I've come to believe that these days, these mind-numbing, never-ending, glorious days of raising small people are the holiest days of them all. They're take off your shoes kind of holy days. These are the days we'll remember, and they're also the days we'll forget.

167

They're the days we wish to end and simultaneously want to last forever. They're sticky and dirty and slow. These are the dog days of motherhood.

I wanted to grow up and do something meaningful with my life. I wanted to do something that mattered and changed the world. I wanted to be somebody. For a while, I wanted to be an astronaut, and then I wanted to be a professional soccer player. I spent a minute wanting to be a missionary and then a nutritionist. I felt like I had finally stepped into my calling when I graduated with a master's degree in counseling. And in a way I had. I had stepped into my calling for a season, and it would be good. What I didn't know then is the Lord can beckon you out of your calling and call you to something else entirely. What I didn't realize then is you can be called to do something you don't really want to do.

I never wanted to stay at home with my kids. We each have our own truths, and this is mine. I always dreamed of daycare or a nanny, of drop-offs and pick-ups, and of business clothes and meetings. I always dreamed of a paycheck. I always dreamed of doing something I was tangibly and noticeably gifted at. But somewhere in the middle of breaking in motherhood, while it still hurt and long before it felt comfortable, God told me to stay. He whispered to me in the middle of the mundane: *Courtney, look up. This is what I have for you right now. I know it's not exactly what you want, and I'm not saying it will be forever but this is what I have for you right now in this season.*

The choice was ultimately mine to make. I could choose what I wanted for myself or I could choose to lean into the tension of obedience and watch what happened next. Motherhood has been an act of obedience for me. And to some degree, regardless of whether you stay at home or work a paying job, motherhood is an act of obedience for us all. We serve our families in such ordinary ways. But our everyday acts of love turn into whispers of the gospel in our kitchens and backyards and around our tables. We are not just doing any work; we are doing the most important work. We are mothering.

I'm finding that I can be so in love with my children and itching to run away and want to stay together and desperate for half a minute to myself. I can want to bottle up parts of their childhood and wish other parts away. I am obsessed with my children and overwhelmed and irritated and infatuated with each of them. I can lose my temper and apologize, and belly laugh all in a day's work. I can long for bedtime and then watch them while they sleep. I love hearing the word "mommy" and hearing it simultaneously makes me twitchy. I am a mother. Exhaustion and grace are my constant companions. Love, not perfection, lives in my home. I have sticky floors, a dirty car, and happy kids. Curiosity and joy run throughout my home. I will live to tell the tales of their childhood. These are the glory days; they are not perfect days, but they are enough. These are the ordinary, extraordinary dog days of motherhood and the God of the universe has declared them to be good.

24

ORDINARY MIRACLES

There's a story recorded in the Gospel of John about a time where Jesus fed five thousand people with one little boy's lunch. The story goes that Jesus was traveling around performing miracles. People would gather, witness a miracle and refuse to leave. Jesus would continue walking, perform another miracle, and people would gather, witness a miracle and refuse to leave. This continues until Jesus has drawn a crowd of five thousand people who are following him because of the miracles they had and continued to witness. Jesus looks up, realizes how large the crowd is and asks his disciples where they can buy bread to feed all the people who have gathered. He asks this as a test. He already had in mind what he was going to do, but the disciples didn't know that;

they were living in the moment.

The disciples are probably hot and tired and hungry. They have been walking with Jesus for who knows how long that day. They most likely just wanted to sit down, take a load off and rest; maybe process the day together. But this crowd has gathered, and now Jesus dares to feed them and on top of that he's asking ridiculous questions. I can imagine hearing Jesus ask this and feeling somewhat exasperated with him. I am not a numbers person, but five thousand people sounds like a lot of people to me. There were no COSTCOs around at the time. Not to mention how much money it would cost to pull that off. Phillip feels my logic because he exclaims that it would take more than half a year's wages to buy enough bread for each person to have one bite.

Another disciple, Andrew, walks up and tells Jesus he has found a little boy who has five small loaves of bread and two small fish. I don't know, but I feel like Phillip might have rolled his eyes at this presentation. Like, well done Andrew but news flash that's not enough. It's funny how quickly we can doubt the miracle worker. Jesus then takes those five loaves of bread and two small fish and feeds five thousand people with them, and there are leftovers. That's the technical miracle of the story; Jesus fed five thousand people with a few loaves of bread and a couple of fish. It's a fantastic story; a childhood favorite if you grew up in the church. But I think there might be another miracle found in this story, too, the miracle of the mom who packed that little boy's lunch.

I can picture her, the woman who stood in her kitchen that morning packing up a lunch for her son. She looked around her kitchen, thought about what her little boy liked to eat and then packed it up for him. She picked up those five loaves of bread and two fish and put them in his lunch box just for him. Maybe she even wrote him a sweet note on a napkin, who knows? But she packed the lunch that morning. She didn't know when she packed it that her lunch would be used hours later miraculously. She didn't know that Jesus Christ himself would take what she had prepared for her son and feed five thousand people with it. She didn't know her lunch would go down in recorded history when she stood in her kitchen doing the work of motherhood. I hope that little boy ran home and told his sweet mom what Jesus did that day.

Packing lunches is so very ordinary. There is nothing all that spectacular about it. It's routine, and towards the end of the school year, it can feel insanely mundane. And it makes me think. Was that mom tired of packing lunches? Did she ever feel unimportant? Did she ever feel unappreciated? Did she ever struggle with feeling bored within the ordinary moments of her life? Was she packing his lunch with a baby hanging off her hip or was another child crying in the background? Were finances tight and scrapping together a lunch felt burdensome? Was she exhausted from being up the night before with a restless child? Did she have laundry that waited for her? Did she kiss him goodbye as she ushered him out the door that morning while one kid hung to her leg and the remnants of breakfast still on the counter needing to be cleaned up? Did she have a child's throw up on her shirt and snot somewhere on her jeans? Had she lost her patience that morning? Did she think what she was doing mattered that day?

But what if that mom hadn't packed her son a lunch that day? What if she had just given him some money and told him to stop somewhere on the way and get a hamburger and fries? Jesus still would have fed the five thousand people, but it wouldn't have been with her lunch. It wouldn't have been performed using her regular offering of love to her family. I love Jesus because he takes such everyday things, like packing a lunch, and turns them into miracles, ordinary miracles. If he can turn a basic packed lunch into an epic miracle for one mom, I have to believe he can do it for me, too. The messy, mundane of daily life might be where our faith lives best.

One afternoon I sat on the floor in a friend's playroom while our kid's played around us as we talked about everything and nothing at all. We started talking about how different everyone is at motherhood, and as we told stories of our children and how we handled different situations it was almost laughable at how much we all differed, and yet every single one of our children was happy and loved and thriving. One of my friends said, "We're all so different at being moms, but we all need each other." And she was right on both accounts.

Sometimes I forget that God placed each one of my children in our home on purpose. He knew before the beginning of time who would reside under our roof and who would not. My family as it is does not surprise him. He did not make a mistake putting my children in my home and not my neighbors. It's not a coincidence that Dustin and I are their parents and it most certainly is not an accident. But sometimes it can feel that way.

I am not crafty or creative. I don't plan elaborately themed birthday parties and all Halloween costumes will be purchased from a store. I cannot draw anything with chalk other than a basic street or maybe a house because it's a square with a triangle on top. Glitter and Play-Doh make me twitchy. I'm not the best at sitting on the floor and talking with Barbie's. I do not care about buying organic foods. My kids like hot dogs and Cheetos, and I am okay with this. Sometimes I struggle to be nurturing. I do not have the patience of a saint. I don't love cooking with my children. And I'm slowly realizing this is all okay because God did not create only one kind of mother and call it good.

He created Jochebed and Pharaoh's daughter. He instilled boldness and audacity in both of them. He dared them to be disobedient for the kingdom's sake. They both had to be feisty. He created Mary who was full of courage. She would step into her calling and raise the son of God and then release him to do what he had been sent here for. He created Hagar who was full of perseverance. When her story became a single mother, betrayed and banished in the desert the Lord saw her. When her best choice was to abandon her starving baby boy under a bush to die the Lord heard the cries and rescued them. She had to be tough. He created Sarah who laughed at God and then tried to deny it. Sarah, I bet she was funny. He created Hannah who was full of resolve. She would beg God for a baby and make a promise she would eventually keep. He created Rebekah who raises twin boys and openly has a favorite son. I bet she was strong, a force to be reckoned with.

God created each one of these women and called them into motherhood. He chose each one to carry the story he wrote for them. God knew each of their stories before one ever came to be. He asked each of them to step into their calling of motherhood on his terms and no one else's. They were not perfect; he didn't need them to be, and yet he chose them anyway. He picked them in spite of their weaknesses and flaws and internal struggles. He wanted them knowing the mistakes they had already and would continue to make. He chose them knowing who they already were and knowing the kind of mom each one of them would be. He knew they would mess up. He knew they wouldn't get it all exactly right, and yet he handed them motherhood anyways.

I'm learning God didn't create me to be everything. He doesn't need me to be everything. He hasn't asked me to die trying to be everything I'm not. Instead, he handed me my specific babies and asked me to raise them. If he had wanted my crafty, precious, patient, organic food buying friend to raise them, he would have done that. I am learning my children don't need a perfect mom they need a joyful one. They need me to show up every day as I am. They don't need me to be anyone else. They don't need a mom who is better at this or that; they need the mom they have to get up every day and walk out confidently the task laid before her. They need a mom who knows she needs Jesus. Because the truth is God knew what he was doing when he handed me this gig, and it would serve me well to put one foot in front of the other like I believe it.

One morning all of my children requested fried eggs for breakfast when the fried egg maker in our home was out running. I turned on the stove, sprayed the skillet and cracked my first egg. Wyatt pulled up a stool to watch and said, "You know mom, it's okay that you aren't the best fried egg maker. You are a really good mom who is good at other things." And that right there is the most accurate thing I have ever heard about motherhood while standing barefoot in my kitchen.

25

LISA

The summer after my freshman year of college I ended up in Honduras for the summer. I was beyond excited and when I got there was the most miserable I had ever been. I still to this day cannot pinpoint what exactly my problem was. The experience itself was great. Everyone was so lovely; Honduras is a beautiful, welcoming culture. But for some reason, all I did was cry and call my mom telling her I wanted to come home. Not surprisingly my mom got tired of this. One day I called her sobbing, and she was done with it. She said to me the following, "Do not call me again. You chose to spend the summer in Honduras, and so you will spend the summer in Honduras. I will not change your flight for you to come home early. If you want to come home, you can figure that out yourself. Otherwise, I will see you in July. Do not call me again. Goodbye." It was a stone cold move.

Instead of taking that phone call as a memo to suck it up and stay the rest of the time I had committed, I took it as permission to figure out my own way home. She had at least given me that option. I approached the director of the place I was interning the following day and told him the truth; I was really homesick and wanted to go home, but my parents wouldn't help me, and I only had fifty dollars on me. He understood. He asked me to sleep on it, and if I felt the same way in the morning, he would help me figure out a way home. The next day we drove out to the airport. We got out of the car and walked up to the window to speak to the woman at the ticket counter where the following interaction took place:

Eddie: Hi, we need to change a flight back to America for free.

Woman: That will not work.

Eddie: Well, how can we change a flight for free?

Woman: You need to be extremely sick with a doctor's note saying you will die unless you are on the next flight out back to America.

Eddie: Okay thank you we will be right back.

We walked back to the car, loaded up and Eddie said, "I know a doctor." A few minutes later we pulled up to a building with people spilling out of it. He told me to wait in the car and that he'd be right back. A while later Eddie came walking out of the building with another man dressed in blue scrubs. I got out of the car, and the Blue Scrub Man said, "You have a severe intestinal issue and if you do not get on the next flight out to America you will die. Do you understand?" I nodded yes, and he signed a paper on the top of our car. We all shook hands and went our separate ways.

We then proceeded to drive back to the airport and speak to the same exact woman we had spoken to a few hours earlier. As we were walking up to the ticket window, Eddie whispered, "You need to act sick." I hunched over, grabbed where I thought my intestines were, grimaced, and made a continual stream of weird sickly noises as they conversed over my doctor's note. The next thing I knew he was ushering me away saying, "You're on the next flight out. It leaves in the morning." *I'm sorry, that worked? My mom is going to be furious.*

I packed my bags, said my goodbyes and headed out the following morning. I chose not to inform my parents about what I was doing until I was in Miami. My mom had told me not to call her again, so technically I was only obeying. I made a tentative phone call to my mother telling her I was in America and would be back in Nashville in a few hours if she wouldn't mind picking me up that would be super helpful. She was stunned and audibly not pleased but showed up at the airport a few hours later, hugged me and drove me back home.

My mom is a gem.

She really is. She is my mom which means I love her so much and I'm also not afraid to admit that sometimes her very existence is too much. Sometimes she breathes or whistles, and I have to physically exit the room and take ten. One day she engulfed me into a hug while I was sobbing in a parking lot over a child and I thought she was the most perfect human alive. But then I met her for lunch one day, and she commented on how much she enjoyed seeing me wearing something other than my yellow Patagonia jacket and all the love I felt for her went out the window.

I wanted to run away once when I was younger. She said that was fine and helped me packed my bags. She even attempted to coordinate my runaway destination of choice which I now understand was for safety purposes. But then she made my favorite dinner, and I chose to stay. My best friend and I broke into the house across the street from ours in elementary school. We were playing an imaginary game and were super into it. We were lost and homeless and desperately needed a place to stay. So we decided to stay in our neighbor's house except we were not invited to do that and also they were not home at the time. The second we opened the door to their house the alarm went off, and we bolted into the woods. She made us apologize later that night. She also laughed about it.

One night in high school I backed out of the garage and ripped the side mirror off of my dad's truck, I texted her from the driveway in a complete panic. She exited the house quietly and helped me duct tape that bad boy back on. She said we'd deal with dad later. She went on strike my senior year of high school. We had driven her insane, and she was done with our shenanigans. For days she did not lift one finger for us. Food, fix it yourself or starve she didn't care. Laundry, figure it out. Transportation, walk or miss it. She was unapologetically not here for any of it. That same year I didn't get asked to prom which always sucks. Instead of building up my self-esteem with words or making me get over it or go with friends, she booked two flights out of Nashville, and we spent the weekend at the beach.

For years she went to bat for me while I battled an eating disorder. I hated her at times, but I'm alive today because she fought for that to happen. When I dropped the food processor blade into my foot and Dustin wouldn't answer his phone, my dad came over to clean up all the blood, but I needed my mom to come back to the ER room with me while I got stitches. She secretly flew across the world to Uganda simply because I asked her to.

When I have a question, the answer is always my mom. *What's my social security number? Where are legumes in the grocery store? How do I cut a butternut squash? Can I send Wyatt to school when he has pink eye? How long do I put my kids in time out for? Can a three-year-old vacuum? How do I get a safe at the bank? How do I potty train? Do you have my birth certificate? How long does it take for meat to thaw? Did we always argue? Did we drive you this insane?*

She is one of the first people I call. She is a good listener and a confidante. She keeps my kids and has dropped everything to come to the rescue of horrible days. She makes us dinner and takes us out to lunch. She's an encourager, and she asks hard questions. At some point, I think I thought I'd grow up and be an adult and not need her anymore. I don't know how moms know everything because I'm a mom and I do not. I thought one day I would magically wake up and know all the answers to everything always. I thought one day I would turn into her. Maybe one day I will, but today I'm thirty-one, and I have three kids and I still very much need my mom. I'm learning that moms never stop being moms;

motherhood is for the long haul. I'm learning there is no perfect way to do motherhood, no perfect way to be a mom. My mom wasn't perfect but looking back she was enough. It has taken three kids for me to look at my mom with more understanding, appreciation, and grace.

My mom taught me that if I want to raise brave kids, I have to be a brave mom. Scared moms raise scared kids. Because of my mom, I want to raise my kids to believe they can change the world and then I want to send them out and watch them do it. Because of my mom, I want to send my kids across the globe, tell them to stop calling me crying, and then I want to be the mom who ends up picking them up from the airport half confused half enamored at the gritty child I have taken part in raising.

26

GOD OF WONDERS

I muttered out to a friend once, "The twins didn't want to come live with us. It's been hard to parent kids who never wanted you in the first place. It's been weird learning to parent kids who are so guarded and mad and scared; kids who push you away and want you and need you and push you away some more all at the same time. Our kids did not choose this life. All of us are growing, and not one of us is the same person we were in the beginning, but sometimes I'm not sure we will recover from how it all started."

I remember waking up one morning in Uganda and fully understanding the magnitude of what we were doing. I looked at Kakuru, and I didn't see the same little boy I had seen the day prior. He looked different, and it wasn't that his body or his face had changed while he had been sleeping, but his eyes had. His eyes looked angry; they looked dark and scary. It was in that moment I knew in my bones he had realized what we had done; taken him away from everything he had ever known, loved and understood. Overnight his eyes had glossed over and gone dead. It was terrifying and heartbreakingly sad. I felt like we had lost him; like he wasn't there anymore and I didn't know if he'd ever come back.

I remember standing in the parking lot of our compound in Uganda attempting to load up the car in order to head to the airport to fly home with the twins when Anita refused to get in. She stuck her almost three-year-old feet into the ground and became a piece of lead. She was unmovable. She locked eyes with me and refused to come with us. I gently picked her up and was met with screaming and thrashing as she lunged for the closest Ugandan and held on for dear life. I had to physically pry her of the body of our friend and put her in the car. She violently sobbed herself to sleep beside me.

We took them away; that will always be where we started. What a crappy ground zero. When much of the world wants to look into the window of adoption and only see the gains and the happy endings the reality is much darker. There is something so twisted about learning to trust and love the people who took you away from all you'd ever known. When you're too young to understand what a family is you don't know even to want one. Learning the art of forever when you know what it's like to be left and taken is excruciatingly painful. Becoming a family does not happen overnight.

Trauma, rejection, and abandonment are all things I'd like to punch in the face sometimes because thank you, Daniel Tiger, but sometimes moms and dads don't always come back. Sometimes love isn't always safe. Sometimes life gives you the middle finger and you, at three years old, are left to figure it out. Sometimes the mom you get the second time around comes and goes for months, moving you back and forth from place to place until it's time to go "home," and after months that turn into years in the same house with the same people, you're still not sure if this is all okay. Because when love hasn't always proven itself to be safe learning how to love and be loved is for crazy people. It turns out fighting for hearts can require some stamina. But love is worth the fight and family is worth marching for. You press forward simply by putting one foot in front of the other. You wake up day after day and continue to choose the act of love. Some days it feels fake and forced and gross; there are moments you wish it were all different. You mess up royally, and you ask for forgiveness, and you keep showing up. Sometimes that's your best meager offering, the gift of showing up. But it turns out showing up might be the most healing thing we can offer. It's easy to show up when you know everything is going to be nice and neat and pretty but showing up knowing everything is going to be ugly and messy and at times complete crap? Sometimes you have to prove yourself to be worthy of the risk of love.

I hit a wall, feeling completely defeated that we had not arrived or made it over this imaginary hump I had created for our family. I desperately wanted to pretend we had all meshed and that we fit so perfectly together. I longed to feel like a mom to all of my children, and I didn't. I ached for healthy relationships with each individual child. I wanted to pretend it felt like we were a family but it quite honestly didn't. The five of us didn't feel right; it didn't feel like we fit together not yet. I wanted to act as if things weren't still so hard and at times awkward. I was tired of how long it was all taking.

One day as I was walking around in my defeated stupor Wyatt engulfed me into a squishy hug and whispered, "I want you to stay like this forever." I had not a clue what he was talking about, but at that moment it hit me straight in the face: we fought for this, him and me. We didn't start right here; we didn't used to be like this. No, we went to battle for tiny moments like this for months that turned into a year we fought for each other's hearts. He and I fought hard for love, and we won; I had to believe I could do it again.

We took family pictures right around this time. It's a funny thing to take pictures of a group of strangers still figuring each other out and label it family. It was an act of faith masked as a stressful Saturday afternoon activity. Family pictures, a declaration of what we are and what I believed we could feel like one day. I went to check our mail one afternoon and found the pictures I ordered sitting there in my mailbox. I turned each one over staring at what the camera had captured. There was one of Dustin holding two smiling, giggling little boys and one of me laughing with Wyatt and Anita. There was one of the boys playing in the leaves together and one of the twins smirking into the camera. I pulled out the last picture and hung it on the wall immediately, the one of all five of us. I stood back after each one had been put into a frame and hung up amazed at what we were doing. Those pictures did not tell the full story as pictures never do but they told a tale my heart had neglected to see. When I looked at my wall, I didn't see anything ugly, messy, forced or awkward instead I saw happiness, laughter, and joy. I saw sparkles in eyes which were once dead and smiles on faces I wasn't sure would ever smile again. I saw grief subsiding. I saw healing. I saw three people who didn't hate each other anymore but rather had turned themselves into siblings right before my eyes. I saw love with my eyes even though I didn't feel it with my heart. I saw a family. The gospel was displayed right in front me on the biggest wall in my home.

Some days I think about that scared little girl who only came with me kicking and screaming; I don't know her anymore. That brave, stubborn girl tells me hourly she is so happy I'm her mommy. She aspires to be a mom, a doctor and a ballerina. I feel immensely proud of her. It still catches me off guard when Wyatt tells Kakuru he loves him; God ordained brothers who once despised each other's very existence. I watch those two boys wrestle and play and laugh together and remember the days I only ached for that to happen. I overheard the twins having a completely broken English conversation about how happy they were here, and I was flooded with relief and gratitude. Some days I think about that boy whose eyes died years ago but have since been resurrected. He was so understandably angry then, and he is so kind today. That boy tells me often I'm his best friend and my heart grows every time it is said.

I sit down at the kitchen table with preschool applications to fill out. I answer the basic questions and then I turn the page. *Tell us about your child.* I scribble down my answers without needing to think. I know my children now. *What does your child enjoy doing?* I run out of space because my children enjoy so many things. *What are some of your child's favorite foods?* I know this one, too. *What are some of your child's strengths?* I have an answer for all three. I close the packet and think about the time my friend asked what I liked about the twins and I couldn't come up with anything. We are not those same people.

Kakuru is brilliant and he is kind. He's a good helper and he wants to do what is right. He is a good friend and he looks out for others. He loves to be outside, he loves to ride bikes and swing and jump on the trampoline. He has an amazing imagination. He loves to play with blocks and the things he builds could go straight to an architect or a designer. He likes to read books and play with action figures. He's a really good eater. He loves macaroni and cheese, pizza, hot dogs, every kind of fruit, and almost every kind of vegetable. Our house is not too keen on zucchini. Chapati, rice and beans will forever be his favorite, though. He will eat anything you give him. Kakuru is a leader, the day he masters the English language he will change the world somehow. He is strong and courageous, he will stand up for what is right and do the right thing even if others aren't.

Anita is smart and funny. She wants to do the right thing but doesn't always choose to do the right thing. She is stubborn. She will make you laugh. She is curious and asks lots of questions. She likes to be in charge and can confidently command a room. She is a good friend. She likes to play with baby dolls and barbies. She is nurturing and compassionate. She loves to color and do anything that involves glitter. She loves to sing and can often be found putting on a concert in the mirror. She's kind of a picky eater. She really likes sugar and desserts, anything sweet. She loves carrots and will always love chapati. Anita is a leader if channeled in the right direction. She could run the world if given the opportunity. She is brave and will do things others are afraid to do. She is strong willed and a fighter.

I like my children, all of them. Some days that feeling overwhelms me. God is in the business of healing and restoration. He is the ultimate miracle worker. He makes ways where there are no ways. He is the redeemer. He mends broken, angry and confused hearts. He turns hate into like into love. He gives sight to the blind and asks lame people to get up and walk. He parts entire seas allowing people to walk right through and turns water into wine. He feeds thousands of people with scraps, and he turns strangers into a family. He is a God of wonders, and he writes really, really good stories if we will only hang on and let him.

27

EBENEZER

I loaded up my car and drove down to Florida with all three kids to spend a week at the beach with my family. We had floats, noodles and every sand toy imaginable crammed into the back of our van. We road tripped hard; the boys peed on the side of the road, I killed a giant spider with one hand while driving, we stopped at Whataburger in Alabama, we cheered every time we crossed a state line, and Wyatt found a way around the dreaded "are we there yet?" question by asking "are we still in Alabama?"

Our last night at the beach we walked down to the ocean after dinner, took our shoes off and I sent my tribe of almost four-year-olds into the water with all of their clothes on. They ran into the ocean squealing with delight. The sun set behind them as they splashed around, dove under the water and tried to fight the waves like ninjas. Eventually, I herded them out of the ocean, we waved bye and told it we'd see it later. As we walked back to the car drenched in salt water and covered in sand Wyatt yelled, "Thanks for letting us play with you!!" I let them strip down and ride naked home much to their amusement.

As I drove home with the windows rolled down, breathing in the salty ocean air one last time; I could not stop laughing. We made it; we had been a family of five stateside for an entire year. We had survived. We did it. I could have cried tears of relief and joy. My weary soul felt a little bit alive again for the first time in a long time; I felt like a weight had been lifted. Something sacred happened in my heart that night on the beach while my kids swam in the ocean with their clothes on with the sun setting behind them. That night will forever be engrained in my mind and embedded in my soul; that night feels incredibly holy to me. It represents so much more than any picture I have of the moment; it symbolizes something so real and incredibly raw- the place we lived to tell about.

A lot can happen in twelve months. A random group of people can indeed begin to turn themselves right into a family. Like can grow from hate and fear can slowly evolve into trust. Grief can become laughter and joy can replace anger. Kids can become siblings. Ashes can become something beautiful if you give it time. My people, I was so incredibly proud of them; proud of all of us. We drove home the following day, gathered Daddy and went out for popsicles. There are certain things worthy of celebrating and surviving a year as a family of five felt like one of the best things we could have ever celebrated.

That fall Dustin and I were gifted an entire week at the beach sans tribe of small children, and it was exactly that, a gift, almost like a wink from God: GO. Before we left I was on the phone with Judy as she relayed details we would need for staying in her condo; as we were hanging up, she said, "I hope you fall more in love with Jesus this week." Falling more in love with Jesus had not been the reason for this trip, and it was not on my agenda for the week, but little did I know I was about to do just that.

I wasn't trying to read Zechariah until another book I was reading mentioned it. I flipped over in my Bible and as the waves crashed in front of me and my toes dug deeper into the sand I devoured the words; absorbed by every one. I starred and underlined; googled for commentary and scribbled in the margins until those pages looked like a complete mess. In chapter nine Zechariah calls God's people, Israel, "prisoners of hope" and as I tossed that phrase around, I found myself entirely undone by what it could represent.

A prisoner is someone who has been captured, taken in and is being confined; they are being held captive. Hope is to expect with confidence and desire with anticipation; hope is to trust. A prisoner of hope, I turned those words over and over in my head and the more I did, the more they felt like an invitation from God to hope all over again years later. I had seen the goodness of the Lord in the land of the living, and he was beckoning me to believe I would see it again if only I kept my eyes on him. Before we left I got it tattooed on my forearm; prisoner of hope, a proclamation that I will see Jesus here.

I was mostly nervous to come home and see our kids; I knew all but one would be excited to see us, to see me. I was especially uneasy about one; the one whose heart was still a little broken and confused. The one whose grief we were still trudging through and most days walking around. The one who was still learning to trust me and the one I struggled to feel love for; the one who wasn't quite sure he loved me. The one who grabbed hold of any opportunity to reject me and publicly choose someone else over me; that was the one I was nervous about seeing. I walked through the gate and could see him through the window of the door. I inhaled and exhaled; bracing for what was to come. I walked up and tapped on the door, he turned around, and his eyes lit up at the sight me. His face gave way to the biggest smile I had ever seen; he stood there clapping and cheering, "Mommy!" He was excited to see me. Never in a million years. I will see Jesus here.

A few months later I found myself sitting on the floor in my sister-in-law's house wrapping up the last of the Christmas presents; filling up stockings and writing names on gift tags when it hit me- we are okay. After living for so long absolutely not okay, it snuck up on me, that realization. I felt at peace, light, almost like the weight of the year and a half prior had evaporated into thin air. I felt like I could genuinely breathe; like life had re-entered my soul. I felt like myself again; I felt happy. God had done and was continuing to do a work inside each, and every one of us and I found myself captivated by it. Redemption was our family's song.

We had marched for family, and a family is what we became. A few nights later Kakuru would whisper into my ear, "I so happy mommy," as I tucked his turtle in beside him and pulled the covers up over him to make him cozy. I would smile and look at that boy and feel a surge of love run through my veins I had never felt before.

Sometimes you have to live through seasons of hate before you arrive at tolerance and sometimes you have to keep pressing on through seasons of tolerance watching it turn into like before your very eyes. Sometimes you have to march for love. Some things in life are only to be lived through; there is no way around it. It turns out sometimes the only way through something is purely through it. Sometimes you must put your head down and do the dirty work of surviving; and then once you realize you have in fact survived you can do the work of remembering, looking back and forging a path forward. Sometimes you have to walk through big, dark tunnels before you ever see a little bit of light signaling the end.

The following summer I would find myself back at the beach with my motley crew of almost five-year-olds. Our last night there we wound up by chance across the street from the spot I think might be my Ebenezer; the place I will always be reminded of what God is capable of, what we are capable of. I let them loose onto the beach, and as they ran into the water, I took my shoes off. I took them off not only because it's stupid to walk in the sand with your shoes on but because it truly felt like holy ground. Watching them that night almost took my breath away. I stood there breathing in the moment before me; letting it saturate my soul and was overcome with God's goodness. He really is who he says he is and the people on the beach that night were living proof. Thus far the Lord has helped us; may I never forget the things I have witnessed here on this earth. He will come down and meet us right where we are every single time; he will show up. He will do a good work, and he will see it to completion; it may look everything and nothing like what we had hoped for or expected but he will do it, and it will be marvelous to behold. My children are miracles, and they are fighters. They are people who have overcome. Each one of them is being restored. What beauty is rising out of ashes and healing is finding its way into their hearts. That little group of rebels, they are my gospel.

28

EITHER YOU TRUST ME OR YOUR DON'T

I don't know if grief ever truly goes away, I think maybe it evolves merely over time. Fear and pain are hard things to shake off when they are your life source. When rejection has been your song, fear and pain are like breath to the lungs and blood to the heart. You need them if you are going to continue living. You can't cut someone off at their life source and expect them to get up off of the table. Fear and pain do not always go away. They are there for a reason, and nobody can take that away from a person. The love of a family does not erase the hurt of your past. The love of another mother does not soften the blow of needing to be loved by the one you aren't with. It turns out you can't always love the fear of your past repeating itself away. A child who is armed with the belief that they, at their core, are unlovable requires you to suit up. So we lock arms, armor up and dance with grief.

Letting someone love you means they can also hurt you. Love makes us vulnerable and when we're afraid to get hurt we build fences around our hearts with no points of entry. We're angry when they can't get in through the door we didn't create for them; we push them away and are mad when they're away, and so we bring them back in. We put spikes on top of the fence around our heart, and we dare them to climb over. We want them to climb over, we know they will climb over and prove to us we are worth risking love for; but they are still the ones who will get hurt first because climbing over spikes always produces blood. Sometimes fighting for hearts can be a bloodbath.

To convince a child who believes they are not worthy of love otherwise is easier imagined than done. Because sometimes for healing to happen we have to receive the one thing we struggle to accept. Sometimes for healing to happen, we have to give the one thing we struggle to hand over. Learning how to connect with a person who cares for you can feel more like hugging a porcupine than a teddy bear. There is nothing soft or safe or comforting about love when you are deathly afraid of it. Quills protect porcupines from danger and sometimes love can, in fact, be a predator. Learning to accept love when you believe you don't deserve it is like running a marathon in quicksand. A person who thinks a blue shirt is actually red cannot be easily convinced otherwise. Dancing with grief is a long, slow, painful dance. You twist, and you turn, and you step on each other's toes. You get blisters, and you make horrible mistakes. You fall down, you apologize, and you get back up. You push away, and you pull each other back in. You dip, and you twirl, and you make something happen. You dance to the beat of grief, and you make messy, beautiful magic.

There was a season I spent walking from bedroom to bedroom in my house praying over each person who slept in it. Sometimes I would move from bed to bed, sitting on each one, taking in the aroma of every one of my children. Often I would proclaim scripture over each, inserting their name, claiming the words to be true in my soul. One morning I walked into the child's room who still often feels like hugging a porcupine. The child who struggles to receive love and the one I struggle to give it to; the one I'm still dancing with. I wandered over to the rocking chair which sits in the corner of the room, sat down and took in the messy bed before me. I took a deep breath, knowing the words I was about to say where harder to say in this room; harder to believe. At first, the words came out in a whisper; the walls couldn't even hear what I was saying.

For you created me in my inmost being; you knit me together in my mother's womb. I praise you because I am fearfully and wonderfully made; your works are wonderful I know that full well. Psalms 139:13-14

He heals the broken-hearted and binds up their wounds... great is our Lord and mighty in power; His understanding has no limits. Psalms 147: 3 & 5

So God created man in his own image, in the image of God he created them; male and female he created them. Genesis 1:27

I repeated these words over and over almost trying to convince myself these words could be true in this room, too. My whisper became audible as I acknowledged these words over my child, over our relationship, over my heart.

Every good and perfect gift is from above, coming down from the father of the heavenly lights, who does not change like shifting shadows. James 1:17

The Lord is close to the brokenhearted and saves those who are crushed in spirit. Psalms 34:18

He will wipe every tear from their eyes. There will be no more death or mourning or crying or pain, for the old order of things has passed away. Revelations 21:4

I reached the end of my list knowing there was one more that needed to be said but I didn't want to say it. I didn't know if I believed this one. Dancing with grief can rub off on you. Fear and pain and rejection can sing in your ears, too. I read the words in my head, keeping them unsaid not sure I could muster them out of my mouth. I read them, again and again, begging my heart to believe them.

As I sat in that chair repeating the same words in my head the Lord whispered quietly to my soul, *you can trust me with this child. I didn't make a mistake here. I know there are days it feels that way and that's okay. I see you; I know this relationship is hard. I know it feels forced and there are days it feels really awkward. I gave you each other on purpose. This is not my perfect plan, but it can still be good. Trust me with this one.* As an act of faith, I whispered the words my heart struggled to believe to be true.

All the days ordained for me were written in your book before one of them came to be. Psalms 139:16

I choked the words out once again, sobs escaping my body and God said to me, *say them again.* Through tears I spoke the words, again and again, every time a little louder than before until I was standing up, pacing the room shouting them at no one but myself and God. I gently felt the Lord say, *either you trust me with this child or you don't.* It's always so simple and so profound.

I stood over my bed sorting mounds of neglected laundry one morning when a child rocketed in flying a LEGO airplane around. With every whoosh! and zoom! I felt the feeling of dread snake its way into my being. I exhaled, commanding the feeling of defeat to leave to leave the room. I looked at the child who is terrified to let me love them and asked where they were flying to. I knew they were flying their airplane to Uganda and that was confirmed. I continued matching socks waiting for what typically came next, the invitation to come along knowing I'd say yes and the internal crushing blow of being immediately uninvited on purpose. But that never happened. Instead, I looked up to see two figurines sitting in the airplane built by the one God asked me to trust him with. God dared me to ask with confidence who was in the airplane that day, and I was kind of pissed. It took a few minutes to muster up the courage, but when I did I was astonished to here, "It's you and me, mommy! We are going to Uganda together this time!" And then we did.

God is love. He is the healer of broken hearts; the one who comforts and the one who restores. He is the one who invites mourners to dance and grievers to laugh. He is the one who invites us to trust him when it makes no sense to do so; the one who asks us to step out of the boat and walk across the water to him. He is the one who loves through us when we can't muster up the strength of our own. He is the one who meets us right where we are every single time and proves himself over again to be exactly who he says he is. He is the one who comes down and slowly but surely removes the spikes on top of the fences around the hearts afraid of love. He will do it; watch him.

29

THINGS PEOPLE SAY

Wyatt and I were headed to the splash pad one afternoon when a little girl came running up to us, pointed at my son and shouted, "Is he yours?" I grabbed his hand, squeezed it and replied with a big smile, "Yep! He is!" She cocked her head to the side and scrunched up her eyebrows, clearly confused but satisfied enough to keep running past us. We put our stuff down, sprayed sunscreen on and jumped into the water. Wyatt was running under a waterfall when she appeared back at my side, "Are you sure he is yours? I mean how does that even happen? You're white, and he's black. How does a white lady have a black baby!?" I stumbled through some awkward answer about how we adopted him and even though we don't look the same I'm still his mom. She shrugged her shoulders and said, "Well my mom is black, and she had all black babies."

Just about everywhere we go our family is on display. We are constantly questioned and prodded and asked to explain ourselves. Strangers feel incredibly comfortable saying just about anything to us. We are regularly asked to explain our family and our children, and not all of the questioning is bad. I do believe a vast majority of people who ask us questions are genuine and simply curious. I also think just because you are curious about someone does not always mean you should ask that someone a question about it. Sometimes, yes, but other times, no. You can be curious and intrigued by our family for days, but that does not mean all of your questions are appropriate to ask. It certainly does not mean all of your questions are suitable to ask in front of my children who have ears and brains and feelings.

It's hard because I want our kids to be proud of where they were born; I want them to love the fact they are Ugandan. I want to allow our kids space to feel whatever the heck they want about adoption while also walking in the security that they belong with us. I want my children to know their story is not up for grabs for anyone and everyone who asks about it. I want to protect them, and I want them to feel proud; it's a fine line at times. I deeply desire to give adoption a good name, but I do not believe it is my job to educate strangers while my children do cartwheels and flips through the spice aisle of the grocery store. I will teach family and friends all day long for as long as I live, but I can't with strangers who I will never see again.

Let's take a few minutes and discuss some of the things that have been said to us by strangers and maybe look at some alternative things we could say to a stranger family you see at your favorite restaurant who does not look the same, shall we?

Are they yours?

Are you their mom?

Are you sure?

Where is the dad?

Look, I want to be kind here, but what if we didn't open a conversation with someone we don't know with any of these questions? It's not exactly thrilling to be picking out bell peppers and have someone ask if you are sure you are your children's mom. Why do you care? You just heard them yell "Mommy" and I am the one who responded. Let's just put on our Assumption Hat here and go with it. What if instead, you said something like, "They are so cute!" or "What a sweet crew you've got there." Ask how old they are or tell me, "Your family is so beautiful!" There are options. Also? Their dad is at work and will be home at five.

Where did you get them from?

Are they adopted?

Did they ship them here or did you go get them?

I know sometimes there is not a better word, but we did not "get" our children from anywhere. We did not purchase them from Target; we, in fact, did not have a coupon for kids. The word "get" sounds like I bought a really cute handbag, and you want to know about it. You do not "get" children because they are human beings. Also, Amazon Prime can do some amazing things, but even they

207

do not "ship" children to your doorstep in two days or less. What if instead, you said something like, "Hey can I ask you a personal question?" or "Do you mind if I ask if your children were adopted?" or "Where were your children born?" or what about, "Did you have to travel?" Any of these would be much more palatable to the passing stranger's ear.

Are you the nanny?

Are you the babysitter?

Do you run a daycare?

Oh, are you guys having a birthday party?

Mom! Look! A black one!

IS THAT A BLACK BABY!?

I am not the nanny, no; there are days I wish I were just the nanny. They are all mine, yes. I do not run a daycare, and we are not having a birthday party. My kids do really like cake if you have any to offer? We are not at the zoo; please stop yelling and pointing. It is a black baby, yes. You, my friend, do not need to attend your next eye exam. 20/20 vision, girl! I do not have any other questions to ask in these cases.

Are you their REAL mom?

Where are their REAL parents?

Why were they adopted?

Do they have siblings?

Are they REAL siblings?

We are their real parents; we are not, however, their biological parents but I feel as if that should go without being said. Last time I checked my children were very much real siblings. No, they are

208

not biologically related if that's what you wanted to know, but their sibling status is very real. Also, their story is not up for grabs at this time, thank you for inquiring. You could, however, ask something like, "Are you sharing any parts of their stories?" or "Do you know much about their history?" and then you'll have to leave it at that when I say we don't share that information with anyone.

Are you going to have kids of your OWN?

Why don't you have kids of your OWN?

Are you having sex right?

Can you just not have kids of your OWN? Is that why you adopted?

Asking another human being in the workroom of your place of employment about their ability to conceive is inappropriate every single time. It's also exactly none of your business. And are we having sex right? Really? Go home. I want to destroy the narrative that tells people the only reason you would ever adopt a child is because you cannot conceive a biological child first. That is garbage and dangerous and hurtful to the children being adopted. This idea tells us that because we couldn't have what we really wanted first we had to settle for something else next. Nope. We chose adoption first, and it has not one thing to do with our ability or inability to conceive; thank you for inquiring.

They are so lucky.

Thank you for saving them.

You guys are so awesome for what you did.

Thank you for what you have done.

These comments are tricky. I understand them, I do, and they are usually well-intentioned. However, adoption is soaking wet with trauma and loss and grief; and that does not make a child lucky at the end of the day. Adoption is often filled with unanswered questions and searching and not knowing where you fit or belong or are wanted. Adoption is not lucky. Even if you mean, they are lucky to have a family or to have us as parents it still isn't lucky to not be with your biological family. I am so thankful for each one of my children and I adore being their mom; and at the same exact time I wish they were living with their moms in Uganda.

I don't have time at the library or the playground to fully explain that we did not save our children from anything. They were loved and cared for in Uganda, and they are deeply missed. There is a person in each one of our children's stories who did physically save them; altering the course of their lives forever and we are not those people. We did not rescue them because there wasn't anything to rescue them from. Their lives are not better now, but instead, their lives are simply different. We did not do anything you cannot do as well. What about "You're doing a great job" or "You guys are great parents."

We were having one of those days where I was asked to explain my family at every turn, and I was not in the mood. We were being asked every last question, and I could see my children processing the reality of each one. I was just over it that day.

Are they your babies?

How?

Why?

Are you their mom?

How?

Why?

Did you adopt them?

Why?

Is that your mom?

How?

Why?

Are they yours?

How?

Why?

Are you their real mom?

How?

Why?

Do you have any of your own kids?

Why not?

Are they real siblings?

Do you know where their real families are?

Are you going to keep all of them?

These questions came at us non-stop for hours. After approximately the 700th time someone asked if I was their real mom Wyatt looked up and yelled, "That is a ridiculous question! Of course, you are our mom!"

Of course, I am.

30

BLACK LIVES MATTER

I met Dustin after work one night at a restaurant by our house. Trayvon Martin had been shot and killed by George Zimmerman almost a year earlier. The jury had deliberated and declared a not guilty verdict; it was announced sometime that week. He was seventeen years old; walking home from the convenience store armed with skittles and his iPhone. He was a black adolescent with his hood on; walking in a community he belonged in and was viewed as a threat. He was seen as suspicious, up to no good and probably on drugs for no other reason than having the audacity to live while in a black body. He was killed because he was black. The picture of him in his hoodie is etched in my memory forever.

At the time of Trayvon's murder, I was not paying attention. I wasn't paying attention because to be very honest I didn't have to pay attention. I was unaware of the unfair treatment of black and brown bodies in present-day America. I was unaware because I didn't have to be aware. Race does not affect me on a personal level, and unfortunately, there are times we don't pay attention to things that don't affect us.

Sometimes I hate that it took adopting a child outside of my race to wake me up. I often wish it were different, but it's not; it's the truth, and the only thing to do with the truth is own it. This verdict; it ripped the blinders off of my eyes and for the first time I could see. It shook me out of my willful slumber and destroyed the safe, white narrative that had been constructed for me. It popped my comfortable, privileged, ignorant bubble right in my face. Trayvon Martin was murdered, and I will never be the same again because of it. That could be our son one day. The sudden reality slapped me hard across the face.

We didn't have kids yet and looking back most days I'm grateful for that. I am relieved we looked up long before we were ever parents and realized how white our world was and how problematic that would be to raise a child who would not be white in. I heard someone say once your black child should not be your first black friend and I am thankful we had time to remedy that. Kids belong in families, yes, but to think we could have brought a child of color into our white world not genuinely understanding how we would need to protect them from it is a little unsettling. What a disservice we could have done.

But that night all those years ago, we sat outside stumbling through our first real conversation surrounding race. It was awkward, and we said the wrong things. It was a messy conversation as we fired questions off at one another and argued over answers. We did not always see eye to eye. We didn't know what we were talking about then but we were talking about it and I have since learned the only way forward is to start right where you are. We sat at that table for hours, but we couldn't stay there forever. We eventually pressed pause on the conversation, got up, drove home and went to bed. I have since learned that being able to table a discussion on race is a privilege and it's what we do next with our privilege that matters most.

We didn't answer all the questions or solve any problems or commit to changing the entire world that evening, but we did commit to not staying right there. We committed to engage and learn forever. We committed to the risk of changing things up in our personal world to better reflect our child. We committed to challenging ourselves, our white people and our community for as long as we live for the sake of our future children.

Since then more names have been added to the already too long list of people of color who have been victims of racism and police brutality. No one is off limits- children, teenagers, adults, men, and women. Their names have turned into hashtags and videos of their last moments on earth have been displayed all over the media. I can now say I have watched people die with my own two eyeballs and it is sickening. To hear gunshots, so many unnecessary gunshots, and watch a person receive those at times resembles a video game. But this life is not a video game; these people are not characters they are sons, daughters, fathers, neighbors, and friends. They are human beings created by a God who sees them and loves them; and on our watches we are allowing them to be abused and murdered, some of the time leaving their dying bodies to bleed out on the sidewalks in front of their communities. Most of the time I stand in my kitchen unable to form words around their mistreatment and murders, I am begging the world to change.

Years later, three Ugandan children under our roof, I remember finding out with the rest of the world Jordan Edwards had been killed by a police officer in Texas. He was fifteen years old and leaving a party with his brother; they weren't doing anything, and yet he is dead today. He was a baby; his face haunted me; I could see both of my boys in his little face. That night at dinner Dustin and I sat at the table talking but not really saying anything about the events transpiring in Texas. Information was still rolling in, and I felt enraged over the blatant disregard for black life that is rampant in this country. We didn't think the kids were listening, but kids are always listening. Wyatt started asking questions with what little he had overheard and could piece together; *What happened in Texas? Who died? What is their name? How did they die? Are they still dead? Can you move your eyes when you're dead? What about your toes? Fingers? Once you die are you always dead? What happens after you die?* Dustin and I looked across the table at each other, took a deep breath and decided to dive in. Every kid is different, and Wyatt could take it in.

I told him we felt sad and mad because a little boy in Texas had died; he had been shot by a police officer, and it was wrong. We told him most people are good; most people want to do the right thing and most police officers are out there doing their job really, really well. They are protecting us, keeping us safe, and making sure people are following the rules, but some police officers aren't doing those things. We talked about how just because you have a job does not mean you are always good at your job. We talked about standing up for what is right and noticing when something happens that is wrong; paying attention to people who are hurting and being activists.

Wyatt wanted to know the little boy's name, and so we said it, Jordan Edwards. He proceeded to say his name over and over again; almost as if he might be able to conjure up his face if he only said it enough times. He asked close to one thousand follow up questions most of which we couldn't answer either because we didn't have the answer or he didn't need to know the answer. Wyatt then asked if he could get down and play; that was that. We had just had a really scary, hard conversation and we were all still standing. As I put him to bed later that night, he asked if we could pray for Jordan's mommy and daddy. With fingers folded together and his eyes shut tight he let out, "God, make Jordan's mommy and daddy's hearts happy. Amen."

It's been so long since we last talked about Jordan Edwards, but every now and then Wyatt will bring it up. It's almost like he's checking in on him; *Is Jordan Edwards still dead? Yeah bud, he is. Do you think his mommy and daddy are still sad? Probably so but I also know they can be happy one day, too.* Now and then he'll randomly educate others about this little boy, Jordan Edwards, who died in Texas and it wasn't okay, and that's why we have to stand up for people and fight for what is right. He also spent months hollering in the car, "Mom! Look! There's a police officer, and he's not dead-ing anyone!!" It was all so very awkward. But he also currently wants to be a "good police officer" when he grows up, so I feel okay about it all.

Changing our narrative is hard; challenging a history that has been fed to us since the beginning of time does not always make sense. Asking questions about history and pressing in on the discrepancies is uncomfortable and not always welcome. Becoming aware of systems of oppression and discovering they have never truly gone away but instead evolved over time is disheartening. Learning about another group of people's dark, painful history is dark and painful. Listening and not saying one word is excruciating. Recognizing I benefit in this world just because I am white, that I have been afforded opportunities my children may not have simply because of skin color is heartbreaking. Having eyes to see and a heart that accepts there are serious discrepancies of freedom for black and brown people in America is at times awkward. Being responsible for my own privilege and therefore my response to my privilege is stretching.

We often walk the line of celebrating our children's blackness and being responsible for teaching them that one day their blackness could be a liability. It's a sobering reality I would not have if I were raising white children. Black lives matter, each and every one. Somedays I want to scream it from the rooftops, and other days I want to whisper it in their ears as if by me affirming it inside of my home the world will follow suit.

31

HEY MAMA

Hey Mama,

It's a random Thursday, and I'm thinking about you. I'm sitting at my kitchen table just having dropped off your babies at school. They're doing well, really well. They talk about you often and are currently really obsessed with the idea that they both grew in your tummy at the same time. Sometimes when I think about you, I wonder if you are thinking about them, too.

I want you to know you birthed two human beings who are incredible. They are five now, and they are phenomenal. They have a brother who is the same age they are; they used to not like each other, but now they do. They are so funny to live with. She is sassy, strong, defiant, and compassionate. He is brilliant, handsome, kind, and the best helper. I think he will launch rockets into space or find the cure for cancer or AIDS. He is the smartest human I have ever known. She is always in trouble. It makes me laugh now, but it infuriates me in the moment. I don't know what to do about it. I was on the phone with my mom for hours just today. She has increased my prayer life that's for sure.

They both have been working hard on mastering the monkey bars. They've just about got it. Your boy has the best laugh. He used to not laugh, but now he does, and it makes my heart swell. Your girl is hilarious. When she's mad at someone she calls them a "dirty penguin," and I'm not even mad about it. She is witty and witty is my favorite.

I want you to know he loves building things with his hands. He can create the most intricate buildings with LEGOS and blocks I have ever seen. He could be an architect someday. She is observant, and she pays attention; she loves asking questions. She touches every single thing in sight and needs to ask a question about it. Sometimes the questions and the touching drive me bonkers, but I think she could be a doctor or dermatologist or a scientist when she grows up. She's a smart one.

I want you to know their favorite TV show is called PJ Masks. Your boy is Gecko, and your girl is Owlette. She loves sugar; cookies, cupcakes, slushies, chocolate, fig newton's, sprinkles, pop tarts; seriously anything that is sugar she loves. The name of her game is my little pony. He loves Batman. He even has a "Batman voice" which is hilarious.

I want you to know she just lost her fifth tooth. I have pulled all of them out myself because my husband thinks he "might be sick" when it comes to pulling teeth. He has lost three and is mad at me because teeth fall out and it hurts. They are both so ticklish, really everywhere but mostly under the arms. She loves anything that sparkles. She is all about some glitter. She is here for shoes, clothes, accessories, and the jewelry and will con it off your actual body if the opportunity presents itself.

I want you to know his eyes sparkle just like his brother's. His eyes died when he left Uganda, and I wasn't sure they would ever look alive again, but they do. By the grace of God they do. The sparkle of those two boy's eyes makes me all kinds of weepy. Your boy is happy now, really happy. She is, too. I want you to know they are brave. They are courageous. They're overcomers, those two.

I want you to know you are loved. You have never been a secret and will never be one. I want you to know we believe in grace, mercy, and forgiveness. I want you to know I can't even imagine having to make the decision you made. I want you know I think you're brave; so brave. I want you to know your kids are amazing, they really are. They are so loved, and they are happy. I'm honored to be one of their moms. I can't wait to show you our kids one day. Thank you for sharing them with me.

Love you, sister.

32

GOD IS HERE

He passed me in the kitchen and whispered, "I want to paint you brown with a paintbrush." He tells me he wants us all to have the same skin color. He wants us all to look alike. He wants a mommy with brown skin. He wants his family to match, to make sense, I get it. It's moments like these I wish my kids had their moms.

Week after week he whispers this to me, "I wish you were brown like me. I want to paint you brown with a paintbrush." It is his first waking thought, the very first thing he says to me in the mornings. He loves me; I know this because he tells me every other minute. This has nothing to do with love.

I look at my beautiful boy, his big brown eyes and sparkly smile, and I tell him it's okay to wish we looked the same. I pull him in close, and I tell him I love him more than any number; I am so glad I am his mom. I hold him tight, and he won't make eye contact, but I see his body exhale as I tell him it's okay to love me and also want your other mom. I kiss his forehead and remind him I am not afraid of his feelings about adoption; he does not always have to like it, and I can handle that.

I'm driving to the park, and I overhear her say, "I wish I didn't have brown skin. I want white skin like you, mommy." It would be so easy to dismiss this statement; say something quick and move on. But my job is to hold space and so I do. "I know you want to look like me and sometimes it's hard that we don't match," I say into the rearview mirror. She nods her head and replies, "But even though we don't look the same, I love my brown skin. I'm so happy you're my mom. I'm so beautiful!" I'm happy I'm her mom, too. And she is right; she is beautiful.

He sits down at the kitchen table and between bites of cereal declares, "I'm so sad that I can't grow up to be a daddy." I take a sip of coffee and press in, "Why do you think you can't grow up to be a daddy, bud?" His answer is genuine, so simple, "Because daddies have white skin and I keep waking up with brown skin." His words shatter my heart into a million pieces, a giant lump forms in the back of my throat. It's moments like these I wish my kids had their dads.

"Of course you can grow up to be a daddy," I tell him. We list off all the daddies he knows who look like he does. We talk about how he can grow up to do and be anything he wants. We tell him again how much we love his beautiful, brown skin. We make a list of all the ways he and his daddy are the same and all the ways they are different. He loves his daddy, and he wants to be just like him, and he will never be.

My sister is pregnant, and he is making sense for the first time that he didn't grow in my tummy. He's never put it all together before. He doesn't understand, and he tells me he's confused; I don't know how to help him understand. He has one hundred unanswerable questions. He cries himself to sleep, and as I close the door to his room, I let the tears stream down my face.

His favorite thing to do is build airplanes and fly back to Uganda. He flies through our home and excitedly tells everyone where he is going. I am often invited and immediately uninvited. He usually doesn't want me to go with him. Sometimes that hurts my feelings, but I pretend it doesn't. He is happy here, or at least happier than he was a few years ago. But there is a Uganda size hole in his heart that will always be there.

We are having Uganda Dinner one night, nothing fancy just the usual. Anita pulls up a stool next to Dustin as he mixes the chapati dough. I ask her if she misses Uganda and she says, "Yes. Uganda was so fun. I want to go back one day." Me too, I tell her.

I am parenting three people who did not want to join our family. They did not choose this life. They did not give their consent, and they did not have a say in the matter. Instead, they were forced to join our family, and they joined it terrified. The Cat in the Hat says you can't be brave unless you're afraid, I think my kids are the bravest.

These people, my people, they are smart. They are funny and mostly kind. They are courageous and strong and tough as nails. They are fighters and overcomers. They are resilient; it runs in their blood. They lost everything in order to gain a family they never asked for. I love my children deeply, and I am so thankful to be their mom. Sometimes I am overwhelmed by how much I like them, and I can't breathe thinking about my life without them. I also wish I didn't know them because in a perfect world they would be living in Uganda with their moms and dads. I believe my kids feel the same most days.

Adoption is beautiful, it really is. It is holy ground. Adoption is also bittersweet and confusing; painful and terrible. Adoption is full of tension. Sometimes I look up at my family, and I feel God whisper, "Do you see me here? This is not my perfect plan, but it is good. Look at what you could have missed out on." And so we lock arms and choose to believe, to hold God at his word; and every time we do God is right there.

Last night we all snuggled up and watched a movie together. We ate dinner on the couch and snorted laughter through *Home Alone*. One of my sons cozied up right next to me and found the spot he fits just perfectly against me. I looked down and smiled. It has taken work to find that right spot, years and years of hard, holy work. I remember when it felt like I didn't know him because I didn't. I remember that time I cringed. I remember when everything was all so awkward. I remember when my kids hated each other. I remember all that screaming. I remember when I wasn't sure if love would ever reside in our home. I recalled the dark, lonely days of parenting strangers I didn't like. Those days are long gone. We know each other now. We like each other now. Day by day our cups are filling up one memory and one funny story and one "I really like this about you" at a time. A group of motley strangers we once were but are not anymore. Last night I looked around at my family, and I believed we were just that, a family. We belong together.

As I type this, my kids are running around in the backyard with their dad. My back door is open because it's warm and December, hallelujah. I can hear him coaching one child in basketball, and he just corrected another child. Two kids are chasing each other. I hear laughter and bikes being ridden. Someone is dressed up as a princess, and I can hear them singing. One child just ran past me to retrieve their jacket because maybe it's not that warm in December. On their way back outside they stopped and did The Floss with a giant grin on their face; I find that dance move equal parts annoying and hilarious. I can hear basketball shots being made and cheers being cheered. Another child just ran through the kitchen to go to the bathroom and stopped and hugged me. I squeezed them tight and told them I loved them; they said it back. I believe us both. *Do you see me here?* I do, yes.

Love lives here. Some relationships still feel forced at times. There are still some days, some seasons, where grief and pain rise up, and they are a force to be reckoned with. One of my children and I are still figuring out how to hug each other; it still feels so weird. Sometimes I will hold a child's hand and burst out laughing at how awkward it is. But love lives here I am convinced. Hope does, too. This is not perfect, but it is good. I see God here.

33

PAINFULLY BEAUTIFUL

The day I went to say goodbye to JT a friend got in the car and went with me. I didn't ask her to come. She knew I was going to do a hard thing and she wouldn't let me do it alone. She told me she was going to go with me and then she did just that. She was there with me while I did the most impossible thing. At one point I remember walking up to her and whispering, "I don't know how much longer I can do this." She took pictures while we played. She got back in the car, and we rode in silence to eat lunch because apparently eating lunch is what you do after you say bye to a child you thought was going to be your son.

Several months later Dustin and I arrived home to a package on our porch. I opened it up and immediately burst into tears; it was the pictures. I had not seen them before. My friend had made a collage of those pictures and put them on a canvas with some words I had written about him. I looked at those pictures, thought about that day and sobbed on the front porch for a good long while. Once I had somewhat gathered myself, I walked inside, found a nail and a hammer and hung that canvas on a wall in our house. It is currently hanging in the hallway of our house now.

It's oddly freeing having pictures from the worst day ever hanging up for anyone to see. I walk by those pictures one hundred times a day. Those pictures that made we weep all those years ago make me smile now. There is something liberating about acknowledging the brutal parts of our story while at the same time recognizing that our life is really beautiful today. Telling the truth is always right. It's hard, but it's still, always right. Honesty always leads to freedom.

I don't know what happened to my little buddy, people always ask. I've heard different things but to be honest, I don't know for sure. We fought for a long time to make sure he would be cared for. Every organization who works with children and families on the continent of Africa most likely has received an email from me at some point. Nobody could help us. He is one of those kids the system didn't work for. He fell through the cracks. We couldn't do anything for him, and I eventually had to let it go. I cannot tell you how painful that realization was for me.

That sweet boy changed my life in a way I never wanted but now am so thankful for. I'm not grateful for him because as a result now I have children and I'm a mom, and everything worked out just fine. I think at some point I would have arrived at being thankful regardless, but I'm thankful for him because at the core he makes me want Jesus. He has stretched me and changed me; he grew my faith. I am a different person because of him. Because of him, I understand suffering, and because of him, I know pain. I am a better person because of him. We are all so afraid of pain. We avoid it at all costs. Suffering? No thanks. The idea of taking a risk is much sexier than actually taking the risk. But discomfort, I have learned, is a teacher. We should welcome it; it is purposeful and powerful.

JT taught me that saying yes is right regardless of the outcome, saying yes is right. He showed me that love does not fit into a box. Through him, I learned that it's okay to do things that scare you. He taught me that sometimes doing scary things will never not be scary and you will just have to do them afraid. Because of him I know I can survive the worst thing ever. My world can crumble right before my eyes, and I will get up the next morning. I will get up because I have gotten up before. He showed me that I am brave. He taught me about grief and pain and suffering. Because of him I now know that grief, like love, doesn't fit into a box. It is a moving, breathing, living thing that comes and goes and changes over time. JT taught me that it's okay to be sad, people may not understand your sadness, but your sorrow is not for anyone else to understand. It's okay to feel. He taught me about permission. He was my teacher on learning how to move forward, that moving forward is not the same thing as moving on. Because of him, I have learned that it is possible to have a beautiful life with a few broken pieces lying in your midst.

He is fine in Uganda. I don't know that for sure, but I believe it. He was strong and kind and brave when I met him, and I believe he is still those things today. His life would not have been better in our family; it just would have been different. Children belong in families, they do, but I believe so hard that children who live in institutions can still be destined for greatness. I have to believe it. He can overcome. He can grow up and change the world. We are more than our circumstances. People overcome every single day. God does not need us to do his work for him, but instead, he invites us to join him in the work already being done. All we have to do is say yes.

I was holding Wyatt walking to the kitchen from our bedroom, and we passed it. He pointed and said, "That's JT, right?" I said yes and proceeded to tell the story of JT to him again. "Before we adopted you we were going to adopt him. He was so funny. You would have liked him. Some hard things happened, and we couldn't do that anymore, so he lives in Uganda still. A little bit later we adopted you, and we're so very happy you are here." He looked at the pictures, looked up at me and said, "I'm happy I'm the one that's here, too." This life, it's so painfully beautiful. All we have to do is say yes and then live the life that follows. Because the best stories aren't the ones that are pretty but rather the ones that are true.

Wyatt, Kakuru and Anita,

We did it. We became the family I wasn't sure we ever would. I'm so proud of you. I'm proud of all of us. You did the hardest thing this world will ever ask of you, and you are all still standing. You're the bravest bunch I have ever had the privilege of knowing. This life is a surprise; it happened right under our noses and was not at all what we expected. Our family is everything and nothing I dreamed it would be. What an honor it is to be your mom this side of heaven. You're my favorites.

Love you,
Mom

ABOUT THE AUTHOR

Courtney Koctar lives in Franklin, TN with her husband and three children. You can connect with her over on Instagram or by visiting courtneykoctar.home.blog. If all else fails, she is most likely standing in her kitchen signing homework folders. Feel free to come over.

Made in the USA
Columbia, SC
17 April 2019